MARSHALL MINI

EARTH

A Marshall Edition
Conceived, edited and designed by
Marshall Editions Ltd
The Orangery
161 New Bond Street
London W1Y 9PA

First published in the UK in 2000 by
Marshall Publishing Ltd

10 9 8 7 6 5 4 3 2 1

ISBN 1 84028 361 0

Originated in Singapore by HBM
Printed in China by Imago

Consultant: Professor Derek M. Elsom
Senior Designer: Siân Williams
Design Manager: Ralph Pitchford
Art Director: Simon Webb
Managing Editor: Kate Phelps
Editorial Director: Cynthia O'Brien
Proofreader: Lindsay McTeague
Production: James Bann
Picture Researchers: Zilda Tandy,
Antonella Mauro

MARSHALL MINI

EARTH

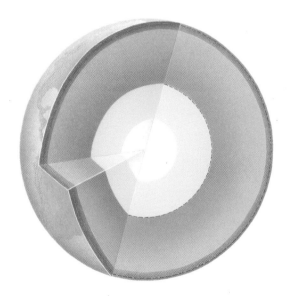

John Malam

MARSHALL PUBLISHING • LONDON

Contents

Planet Earth 6

Earth's structure 18

Restless Earth 36

Weather and climate 68

Earth's gifts 80

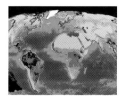

Mapping, measuring, exploring 92

Fact file 100

Glossary 112
Index 116
Useful addresses 120
Acknowledgements 120

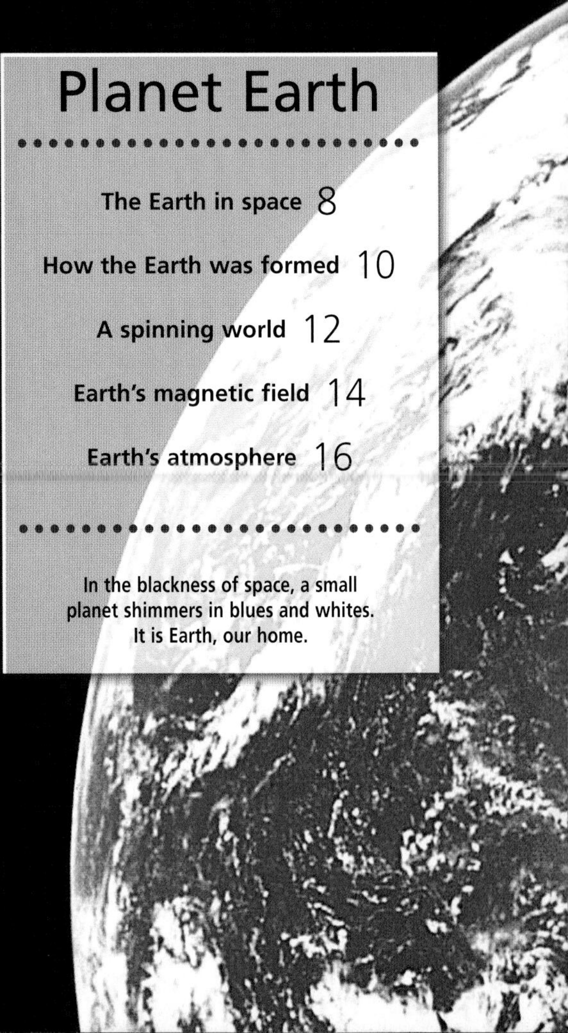

Planet Earth

The Earth in space 8

How the Earth was formed 10

A spinning world 12

Earth's magnetic field 14

Earth's atmosphere 16

In the blackness of space, a small planet shimmers in blues and whites. It is Earth, our home.

The Earth in space

The Earth is a small planet. It belongs to a family of planets that exist close to a star we call the Sun. They form part of a body in space called a galaxy, which is one of billions in the universe.

Solar system and the planets

Our solar system is the Sun, nine planets, more than 60 satellites (or moons), more than 5,000 asteroids and numerous smaller objects such as comets, dust and debris. The Sun is the largest body and the planets and other objects travel around it.

Mercury – diameter: 4,979 km
distance from Sun: 58 million km

Venus – diameter: 12,104 km
distance from Sun: 108 million km

Earth – diameter: 12,756 km
distance from Sun: 150 million km

Mars – diameter: 6,794 km
distance from Sun: 228 million km

Jupiter – diameter: 142,984 km
distance from Sun: 778 million km

Saturn – diameter: 120,536 km
distance from Sun: 1,430 million km

The Sun

The Sun is the nearest star to the Earth. It is a mass of hydrogen and helium gases. The Sun makes huge amounts of heat and light. It takes about eight minutes for the Sun's light to reach the Earth.

At 6 billion years old, the Sun is about half way through its life.

The Milky Way Galaxy

Our Sun in the universe

The universe is everything that exists, including all the space in between the objects. Within the space are clusters of stars called galaxies. Our Sun is one of billions of stars in the Milky Way Galaxy, which is shaped like a spiral.

Clusters of stars in galaxies

Uranus – diameter: 51,118 km
distance from Sun: 2,870 million km

Pluto – diameter: 2,274 km
distance from Sun: 5,915 million km

Neptune – diameter: 49,532 km
distance from Sun: 4,500 million km

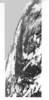

How the Earth was formed

About 12 billion years ago the universe exploded into existence. This moment of creation is called the Big Bang. The universe expanded out from a single point and is still expanding today.

The age of the Earth

The Earth is about 4.6 billion years old. At the start of its life it existed as a globe of molten rock. Gradually, the rock on the surface cooled down to form a hard outer layer, or crust. But beneath the young planet's thin skin, its inside layers remained as liquid rock and metal. Gases came from inside the Earth and made clouds. Rain fell from the clouds and made the oceans.

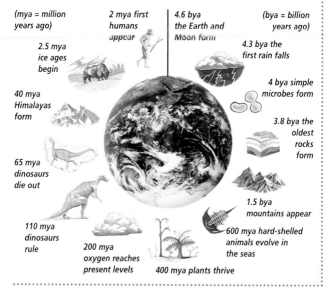

(mya = million years ago)

2 mya first humans appear

4.6 bya the Earth and Moon form

(bya = billion years ago)

2.5 mya ice ages begin

4.3 bya the first rain falls

40 mya Himalayas form

4 bya simple microbes form

3.8 bya the oldest rocks form

65 mya dinosaurs die out

1.5 bya mountains appear

110 mya dinosaurs rule

600 mya hard-shelled animals evolve in the seas

200 mya oxygen reaches present levels

400 mya plants thrive

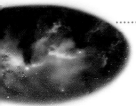

The solar system formed inside a swirling cloud of gas, ice and dust.

Birth of the solar system

The Sun and planets were born out of a cloud of gas, ice and dust. As the Sun formed, its gravity pulled the debris into clumps. The clumps grew bigger until they formed the planets.

A central mass formed inside the cloud. Around the mass were lumps of gas, ice and dust (right).

The central mass became the Sun (above left). The lumps became the planets (above).

The solar system was born, with all the planets moving in the same direction around the Sun.

A spinning world

The Earth does not stand still. It spins fast around its axis while moving slowly around the Sun. This motion causes night, day and seasons.

Foucault's pendulum

A French physicist, Jean Foucault (1819–68), used a pendulum to show the Earth's spin. When the pendulum was released it swung along a marked line. After several hours it seemed to have changed direction, but it was really the Earth that had turned.

Pendulum

Marked line

The changing seasons

Because the Earth tilts towards the Sun, places move nearer and then further from it during the year. This means the amount of light and heat they receive increases and decreases as the Earth travels around the Sun, so the weather changes and seasons occur. Places between the equator and the poles have spring, summer, autumn and winter seasons. The poles have only summer and winter.

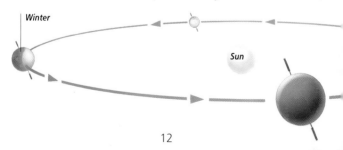

Winter

Sun

Lands of the midnight Sun

In places near the poles, such as northern Norway, the Sun never sets for about six months of the year, as these photographs taken over 24 hours show. The Sun can still be seen at night, since it stays just above the horizon.

Spin and tilt of the Earth

The Earth spins around once in 24 hours. Places at the equator move at over 1,600 kilometres per hour; those at the poles hardly spin at all. The Earth spins eastwards, so the Sun seems to rise in the east and set in the west. The Earth tilts towards the Sun at an angle of 23.5 degrees. The angle is measured from an imaginary line between the poles, called the axis.

Direction of spin

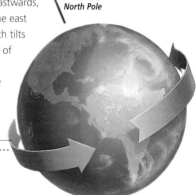

North Pole

Axis

South Pole

Summer

Summer happens in Earth's northern region, or hemisphere, when the North Pole tilts to the Sun. Winter happens when it tilts away.

13

Earth's magnetic field

An invisible force field cloaks the Earth with magnetism. As particles from the Sun charge towards us, the magnetic field deflects them. Those that get through light up the night sky.

The teardrop-shaped magnetosphere

The Earth's magnetosphere, or magnetic field, surrounds the planet and extends 60,000 kilometres into space. It is generated by the molten iron of the Earth's outer core. The magnetosphere protects the Earth from the Sun's harmful solar wind particles, which travel at up to 2,000 kilometres a second. As the particles hit the magnetosphere they slow down. Some are drawn towards the magnetic North and South poles, where they produce auroras.

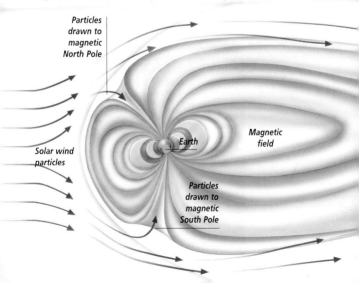

Particles drawn to magnetic North Pole

Solar wind particles

Earth

Magnetic field

Particles drawn to magnetic South Pole

Magnetic poles

Molten iron in the Earth's outer core makes an electric current. The current produces electricity, which creates a magnetic field. The field has end points that lie close to the North and South poles. These two points are the magnetic poles.

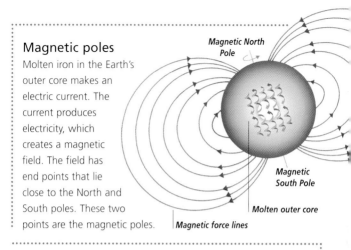

Magnetic North Pole

Magnetic South Pole

Molten outer core

Magnetic force lines

Auroras – lights in the sky

Near the Earth's poles, colourful lights shimmer in the night skies. They are called auroras. The *aurora borealis* (northern lights) is seen near the North Pole and the *aurora australis* (southern lights) near the South Pole. They are caused by the solar wind – a stream of particles that reacts with gases in Earth's upper atmosphere.

The *aurora borealis*, seen in the northern night sky

15

Earth's atmosphere

The atmosphere is essential for the survival of all life on the Earth. It provides us with oxygen to breathe, blocks out rays from the Sun, which can harm us, and keeps the weather in.

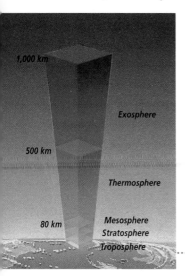

1,000 km

Exosphere

500 km

Thermosphere

80 km

Mesosphere
Stratosphere
Troposphere

Atmosphere layers

The Earth's atmosphere extends about 1,000 kilometres above the surface of the planet. It is divided into several layers. All living things and the weather are contained in the lowest layer, the troposphere. This layer averages about 10 kilometres in height – it is thinner at the poles and thicker at the equator. Gases in the layers trap the Sun's heat and keep the Earth warm.

The air we breathe

Today's atmosphere is made up of about 76 per cent nitrogen gas and 21 per cent oxygen gas. The remaining 3 per cent is a mixture of other gases such as argon, carbon dioxide, neon, helium and methane.

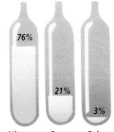

76%

21%

3%

Nitrogen Oxygen Others

The Earth's early atmosphere was a mixture of methane, carbon dioxide and hydrogen sulphide gases.

Rain fell and made the oceans. They were rusty-brown in colour since the water reacted with the Earth's iron.

Chemicals in the oceans made amino acids, from which came the first signs of life – bacteria (see inset, which is much magnfied).

Formation of the Earth's atmosphere

For its first billion years, the Earth's atmosphere was a mixture of poisonous gases. About 3.5 billion years ago, bacteria – the first life – appeared in the oceans. They grew into tiny plants, called algae, that gave off oxygen gas. This gas gave the Earth its breathable atmosphere.

Oxygen filled the oceans and made the atmosphere breathable. New life forms could begin.

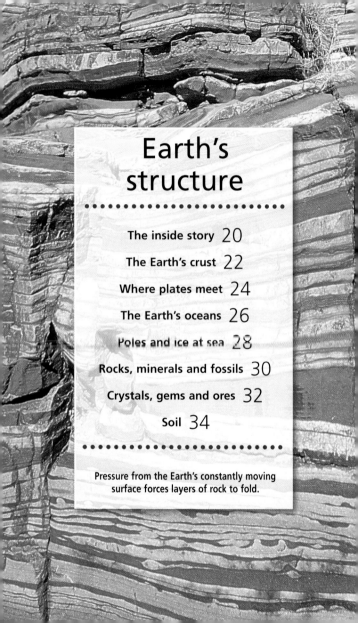

Earth's structure

The inside story 20

The Earth's crust 22

Where plates meet 24

The Earth's oceans 26

Poles and ice at sea 28

Rocks, minerals and fossils 30

Crystals, gems and ores 32

Soil 34

Pressure from the Earth's constantly moving surface forces layers of rock to fold.

The inside story

Earth has many layers, from its outermost rocky skin on which we live to its innermost iron heart. The layers below the surface hold secrets about the planet, but they are too hard and hot to reach.

The Earth's layers

Earth's thin outer layer is the crust. The layers below it are out of reach, and it is by studying earthquake shock waves that we know about them. The mantle is made of minerals such as magnesium and iron, and molten rock called magma. The core is mainly iron, the outer part is liquid and the inner is solid. It is 5,000°C at the centre – as hot as the Sun's surface.

Inner core
1,280 km thick

Outer core
2,250 km thick

Mantle
2,900 km thick

Crust
32 km thick on average

Thin crust under oceans

Features of the crust

The crust is Earth's skin, a layer of solid rock on which we live.
On average it is about 32 kilometres thick. It is thickest under
the continents, where it bulges down to a depth of
up to 65 kilometres. It is thinnest under the
oceans, where it is just 8 kilometres thick.
Its surface is marked by mountains,
plains and trenches.

Older mountains

Young fold mountains

Interior plains

Deep sea trench

Thick crust under continents

Deepest mine 3.8 km

Deepest sea trench 11 km

Deepest geological exploration 15 km

Holes in the crust

It is about 6,400 kilometres to the
centre of the Earth, yet the greatest
depth reached so far is 15 kilometres – a borehole in
Russia. In South Africa a gold mine is at 3.8 kilometres.
The Marianas Trench in the Pacific Ocean is the lowest
natural point on Earth – 11 kilometres below sea level.

The Earth's crust

The crust is never still. Long ago, all land on the Earth belonged to one huge mass, over which animals freely roamed. But the mass broke up and pieces drifted away.

250 million years ago all the Earth's land was joined in one huge mass. This supercontinent has been named Pangaea, meaning "all lands".

About 200 million years ago Pangaea began to break up. By 135 million years ago it had divided into two main landmasses, Laurasia in the north and Gondwana in the south.

Pangaea

Tethys Ocean

One super-continent

Laurasia

Tethys Ocean

Gondwana

The super-continent breaks up

North America

South America

Smaller continents appear

Emergence of today's continents

The Earth's continents have moved into place by tiny movements of the Earth's crust. The crust is cracked into giant pieces, called plates. They float on the molten rock, or magma, of the mantle, which is the layer immediately below the crust. As magma breaks through the crust and comes to the surface, it forces plates to move. It has taken millions of years for this never-ending process to move the continents to where they are today. It is called continental drift.

Fossils are clues to joined-up continents

We know that the continents were once joined because fossil remains from the same animal species have been found in many parts of the world. For example, fossils of the dog-sized *Lystrosaurus*, which lived 220 million years ago, have been found in Asia, Africa, South America and Antarctica. It was free to roam where it liked since there were no oceans to get in its way.

Lystrosaurus

Laurasia and Gondwana slowly broke apart until, by 65 million years ago, the familiar outlines of today's continents had started to take shape.

As the continents continued to move, they drifted into the positions they are in today. They are still moving at between 1 and 4 centimetres a year.

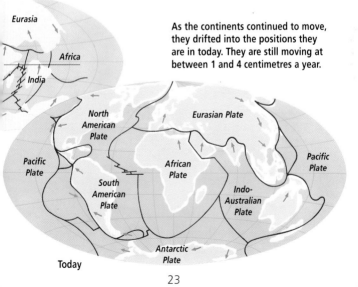

Eurasia

Africa

India

North American Plate

Eurasian Plate

Pacific Plate

African Plate

Pacific Plate

South American Plate

Indo-Australian Plate

Antarctic Plate

Today

Where plates meet

Where plates meet, lines of weakness occur in the Earth's crust. The crust comes under great pressure at plate boundaries, where the massive slabs of rock push, pull and slide against each other.

Deep ocean trenches form in places where one plate sinks under another. Huge earthquakes happen here.

Where two plates slide by each other, a crack is made called a fault line. Major earthquakes occur along fault lines.

When two plates ram into each other, the crust buckles from the pressure and is pushed up as mountains.

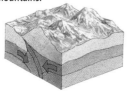

As plates under the sea slide away from each other, magma rises up along the split and hardens into mid-ocean ridges.

Plates meeting and moving

Where two plates come together, they collide, move apart or slide past each other. Each plate grows along one edge as new material is added to it from inside the Earth. The other edge is destroyed by sinking back into the Earth or rising up as mountains.

The San Andreas Fault in California, USA, marks the boundary between the Pacific and North American plates.

Boundaries of the Earth's crustal plates

The crust is a jigsaw of about 7 large and more than 12 small plates. They move in different directions and at varying speeds. Most are under both land and sea. Some are only under the sea.

The sea floor spreads

The sea floor is always moving. The process begins at an ocean ridge, where magma rises to the surface. From there it spreads outwards, cooling down and hardening into new crust. At an ocean trench it slides under an adjoining plate and is melted back into magma.

| Ocean trench | Sea floor spreads out | Ocean ridge | Melting crust |

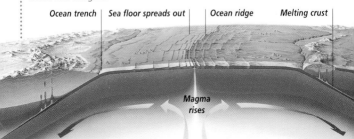

Magma rises

The Earth's oceans

Oceans cover more than two-thirds of the Earth. Beneath their salty water, the crust rises and falls, just as it does on land, creating a landscape that we are only now beginning to explore.

Exploration of the oceans

Diving vehicles, called submersibles, explore the ocean's depths. Some carry a crew of two or three people. Others are unmanned robots, which are controlled from a command ship on the surface.

Features on the ocean floor

The edge of a continent slopes under the ocean to form a continental shelf. Beyond the shelf the ocean floor drops steeply away. Between the continental shelf and mid-ocean ridge is a flat area known as the abyssal plain. Where the Earth's crustal plates meet, ocean trenches form. Undersea mountains are seamounts.

Continental shelf | *Abyssal plain* | *Mid-ocean ridge*

Black smokers

Where the sea floor spreads out along an ocean ridge, chimneylike stacks of minerals form above holes in the crust, called vents. Water, heated to 400°C, gushes from the stacks, bringing with it minerals from inside the Earth. The minerals settle on the stacks and make them grow. Sulphur turns the water black, so the stacks have been named black smokers.

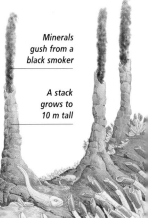

Minerals gush from a black smoker

A stack grows to 10 m tall

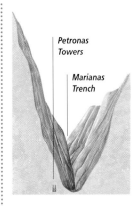

Petronas Towers

Marianas Trench

Marianas Trench

A depression on the floor of the Pacific Ocean, west of the Philippines, is the deepest known point on the Earth's surface. This is the Marianas Trench, an 11-kilometre-deep chasm. In 1960, a two-man American navy submersible descended to the bottom of the trench. The world's tallest building, the Petronas Towers (Kuala Lumpur), is dwarfed by the trench.

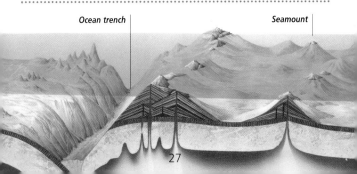

Ocean trench

Seamount

Poles and ice at sea

The Earth's poles lie amid frozen wildernesses. Snow that falls at the South Pole becomes an icy sheet that grips the land, while freezing temperatures at the North Pole turn the sea to ice.

North and South poles

The North and South poles are at either end of Earth's axis, which is the invisible line around which the planet spins. They are the planet's geographical poles, or points, and they lie opposite each other. Their positions are fixed, unlike the nearby magnetic poles, which can and do change position with time.

The Arctic

North Pole

Greenland

Antarctica

● South Pole

The North Pole is surrounded by the Arctic, a region of sea ice floating on the Arctic Ocean. In winter the sea ice extends to cover a larger area.

The South Pole is surrounded by the continent of Antarctica, a rocky land covered by a layer of compressed snow called an ice sheet. In some places the ice is 5 km thick.

Sea ice

During the bitterly cold winters at the poles, the sea freezes over when its temperature falls below −1.9°C. Sea water freezes into sea ice, which floats on the surface. Most sea ice is never more than about 2 metres thick.

Ice breaker ships push through sea ice, keeping channels open for other ships.

Icebergs

An iceberg is a floating mass of ice, found in the seas around the poles at places where glaciers and ice sheets reach the coast. As the ice enters the sea, chunks break off and drift away as icebergs. Arctic icebergs (below) are usually tall with an uneven, angular shape. Antarctic icebergs are flatter and more blocklike in shape.

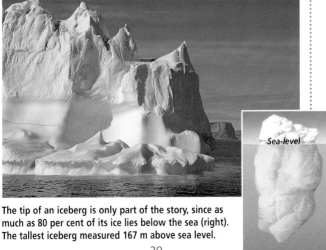

Sea-level

The tip of an iceberg is only part of the story, since as much as 80 per cent of its ice lies below the sea (right). The tallest iceberg measured 167 m above sea level.

Rocks, minerals and fossils

Rock is the material of the Earth's crust. All rock is made from chemicals, called minerals, which group together. When minerals replace the bones of dead animals with rock, fossils are made.

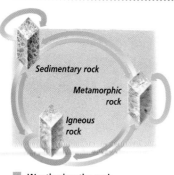

Sedimentary rock

Metamorphic rock

Igneous rock

■ Weathering the rock
■ Pressuring the rock
■ Melting the rock

The rock cycle

The process of changing, or recycling, one type of rock into another is called the rock cycle. By various processes – such as melting, weathering and pressuring – the three classes of rock change from one to another. The same processes even change them into new forms of themselves. The cycle never stops.

Fossil formation

An animal fossil forms when a creature falls into mud or sand and is covered by sediment (tiny grains of solid material). The sediment hardens to stone around the creature. Its skeleton rots away to leave a print of its bones in the sediment. This is a mould fossil. If the mould fills with sediment, a cast fossil is made. It looks like the real skeleton.

A fish dies and sinks to the seabed. Its soft parts decay but its bones remain.

30

Rock types and layering

There are three types of rocks: igneous, sedimentary and metamorphic. Igneous rock is formed from magma (molten rock). Sedimentary rock is made from pieces of weathered rock, called sediments, which are compressed into layers. Metamorphic rock begins as igneous or sedimentary rock but is forced by heat or pressure to change (metamorphose) into another rock type.

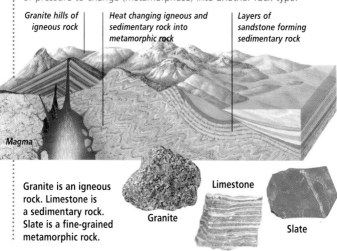

Granite hills of igneous rock

Heat changing igneous and sedimentary rock into metamorphic rock

Layers of sandstone forming sedimentary rock

Magma

Granite is an igneous rock. Limestone is a sedimentary rock. Slate is a fine-grained metamorphic rock.

Granite

Limestone

Slate

Sediment covers the bones. Minerals slowly replace the bones and harden into rock.

Movements in the land lift the fossil out of the water and on to dry land.

As the land is slowly weathered away, the cast of the fossil skeleton is revealed.

Crystals, gems and ores

Minerals are the building blocks of the rocks we call crystals, gems and ores. Created by the processes that formed the Earth, they are valued for their many practical and decorative uses.

Cubic: diamond, galena

Hexagonal and trigonal: emerald

Triclinic: turquoise

Monoclinic: gypsum, azurite

Tetragonal: zircon

Orthorhombic: sulphur, topaz

Crystal systems

Most minerals make shapes called crystals. Each of these minerals has its own special shape, known as a crystal system. The shapes are based on the angles crystals make at their corners, together with the lengths of any three sides. There are six basic crystal shapes (see left). Most crystals have a specific colour, such as sulphur, which is yellow.

Mineral gemstones

Most gemstones are minerals. They are crystals which, when cut and polished, are highly prized. Many, such as diamonds, emeralds and rubies, are rare and expensive and are called precious stones. Others, such as opals, are more common and are semiprecious stones.

Uncut diamond in rock

Ore-bearing minerals and pure ores

Some minerals are called metals, most of which are found in the ground in mixtures called ores. Pure ores, also called native metals, are metals that are found as solid lumps, such as gold. After mining, ores are crushed and melted to extract the metals.

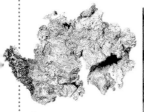

Copper occurs as a pure ore since it is found on its own and is not mixed with other minerals. It is a metal with many uses.

Open-cast mining for tin, in Brazil

Cut ruby

Uncut ruby

Cut diamond

Organic gemstones

Not all gemstones have a mineral origin. Some are formed from plants or animals, which is why they are termed organic. Amber (fossilised tree resin), pearl, shell and jet are all examples.

Amber

Soil

Soil is the thin fertile layer on the land in which plants grow. It is a mixture of minerals, organic matter, air and water. It forms through weathering and the actions of plants and animals.

How soil forms

In the first stage, parent rock breaks down into mineral particles. Lichens and mosses grow and water seeps down. An immature soil forms. The next stage is a young soil. Grasses and shrubs grow and create a layer of organic litter, which enters the soil. In the final stage, mature soil forms from the mixing of organic and mineral materials.

Immature soil

Parent rock

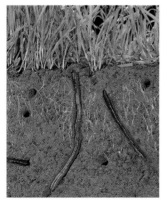

Earthworms improve soil

By passing organic matter and soil through their bodies, earthworms break minerals into tiny particles, or grains. They deposit them as casts, which improve soil structure. Earthworm burrows aid drainage and improve aeration, allowing air to enter into the soil.

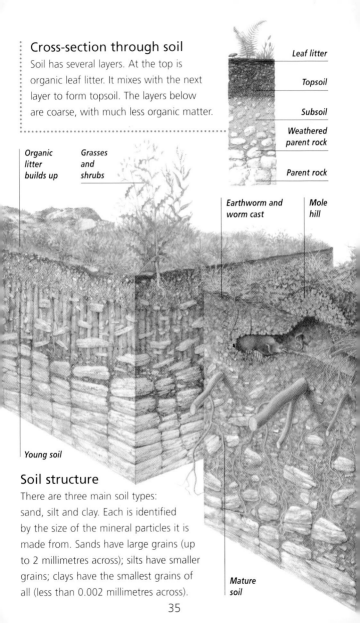

Cross-section through soil

Soil has several layers. At the top is organic leaf litter. It mixes with the next layer to form topsoil. The layers below are coarse, with much less organic matter.

Leaf litter

Topsoil

Subsoil

Weathered parent rock

Parent rock

Organic litter builds up

Grasses and shrubs

Earthworm and worm cast

Mole hill

Young soil

Soil structure

There are three main soil types: sand, silt and clay. Each is identified by the size of the mineral particles it is made from. Sands have large grains (up to 2 millimetres across); silts have smaller grains; clays have the smallest grains of all (less than 0.002 millimetres across).

Mature soil

Restless Earth

Waves and tides 38

Coasts 40

Islands and atolls 42

Mountains 44

Glaciers 46

Rivers – the upper course 48

Rivers – the lower course 50

Valleys 52

Lakes 54

Caves 56

Sand deserts 58

Deserts and oases 60

Volcanoes 62

Volcanic landscape 64

Earthquakes 66

Earth's restless interior continues
to shape the surface of the planet.

Waves and tides

The oceans are in constant motion. Wind ripples their surface and makes waves, while twice every day the tide washes in and then falls back.

Wave formation

Waves form as wind blows over the sea. As a wave travels towards the land, water particles inside it move around in circles, rising up into crests and sinking down into troughs. Near the coast the motion becomes less circular. The waves slow down, their crests curve over and they break on to the shore.

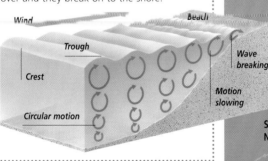

Wind

Beach

Trough

Crest

Circular motion

Wave breaking

Motion slowing

Day 1
Spring tide
New moon

The Moon and the tides

The Moon's gravity pulls the oceans towards it. Its pull forms a bulge of water on the side of the Earth nearest the Moon, and another on the opposite side. The bulges of water follow the Moon as it circles the Earth, making the tides.

The tide cycle

The tides follow a 28-day cycle, linked to the positions of the Earth, Moon and Sun. At full and new Moon, the Moon and Sun line up with the Earth. The extra gravity from the Sun pulls even more on the ocean and a high (spring) tide occurs. Low (neap) tides occur when the Sun and Moon do not line up.

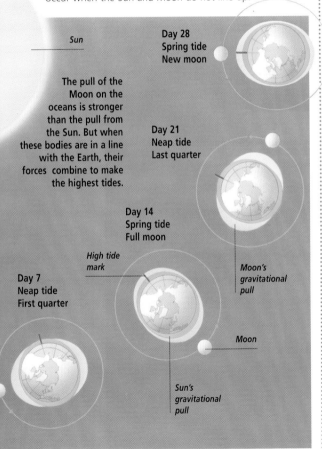

Sun

**Day 28
Spring tide
New moon**

The pull of the Moon on the oceans is stronger than the pull from the Sun. But when these bodies are in a line with the Earth, their forces combine to make the highest tides.

**Day 21
Neap tide
Last quarter**

**Day 14
Spring tide
Full moon**

High tide mark

**Day 7
Neap tide
First quarter**

Moon's gravitational pull

Moon

Sun's gravitational pull

Coasts

The coast is where land and sea meet. It is worn into shape by the pounding action of waves. The coastline continually changes as the sea is always wearing the land away, in a process called erosion.

Development of coastal features

The coastline is the result of non-stop erosion. Bays and arches form when soft rock is worn away by the sea, leaving harder rock to stand as headland cliffs and towerlike stacks. As wave action wears rocks down into smaller and smaller particles, and as rivers carry loose material to the coast, the sea moves the material along the shore and piles it up into beaches. Beach material can be moved sideways by the sea to form sandy spits and bars.

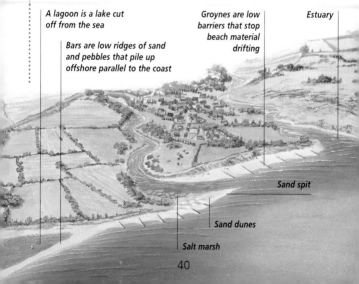

A lagoon is a lake cut off from the sea

Bars are low ridges of sand and pebbles that pile up offshore parallel to the coast

Groynes are low barriers that stop beach material drifting

Estuary

Sand spit

Sand dunes

Salt marsh

Coastal erosion

The process that shapes the coast is erosion. Waves hurl pebbles and rocks against the shore, increasing the cutting power of the sea. Air is squashed into cracks in the rocks, and when a wave pulls back, the air explodes, bursting the rocks apart. Chemicals in seawater dissolve soft rocks, such as chalk and limestone.

Erosion has worn away soft rock to make an arch, on the south coast of England.

Beach

Bay

Arch

Stack

Headland

Sea cave – water sprays up through a blow hole in the cave roof

Waves erode a crack in a headland, enlarging it into a sea cave. If erosion occurs on both sides of the headland, the cave opens up into an arch. When the cave roof falls, a stack is left standing.

Islands and atolls

Scattered across the oceans are patches of dry land called islands and atolls. Some are the result of the sea level rising, others have been made by volcanoes or are the work of sea creatures.

Continental islands

Islands can form in many ways. Continental islands were once part of a nearby landmass, or continent, but became separated from it over time. Erosion, a rising sea level and the movement of the Earth's plates can all leave land isolated as islands.

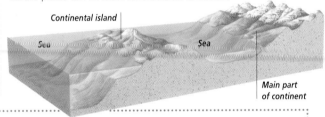

Continental island

Sea

Sea

Main part of continent

Rising sea level

Large areas of the Earth's surface were once covered in ice. As the ice melted, some 10,000 years ago, the sea level slowly rose and flooded low-lying land. High ground remained above sea level and formed islands cut off from the mainland.

As low-lying land floods, islands form.

42

Volcanic islands

Where crustal plates collide, volcanic islands emerge along arcs, such as the islands of Indonesia. The chain of Hawaiian Islands lies above a volcanic hot spot, which burns through a moving plate. Where plates pull apart, new islands form as magma rises.

A new island, Surtsey, near Iceland, emerged during a volcanic eruption.

Formation of an atoll

An atoll is a ring-shaped coral reef around a lagoon of shallow water. Most atolls form in clear, tropical sea, where corals flourish. Atolls begin as fringing reefs, often around a volcanic island. As the seabed subsides, the island slowly sinks, but the coral reef continues to grow upwards. An atoll is the final stage of a reef, where the land disappears under the sea to leave a ring of coral.

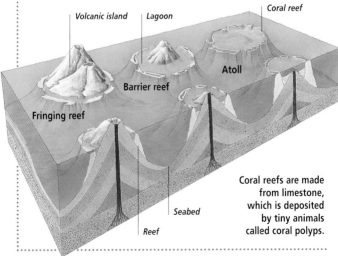

Volcanic island *Lagoon* *Coral reef*

Atoll

Barrier reef

Fringing reef

Seabed

Reef

Coral reefs are made from limestone, which is deposited by tiny animals called coral polyps.

Mountains

Mountains are masses of land that rise high above their surroundings. They occur in ranges, which can extend for thousands of kilometres and which take millions of years to form.

Mountain building

There are three stages in the creation of a typical mountain range. First, sediment is washed off the land by rivers or thrown out by volcanoes. The sediment builds up in thick layers, usually in the ocean, where it is compressed into sedimentary rock. Second, movements of the crust put the rock under pressure, forcing it to fold. Third, there is a period of uplift, when pressure pushes the rock up as mountains.

Asia

Ocean

India

India

World's tallest mountain

Mauna Kea, which means "White Mountain", is a dormant volcano on the island of Hawaii. From the seabed to its summit it measures 9,754 metres, making it both the highest island mountain and the tallest mountain in the world – taller even than Mount Everest.

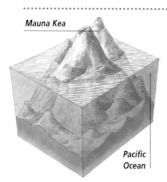

Mauna Kea

Pacific Ocean

Block and dome mountains

Movements of the Earth's plates put layers of rock under such pressure that they crack along lines, called faults. Steep-sided block mountains form along faults where slabs of rock are forced up. Dome mountains, which have smooth sides, are pushed up by rising magma.

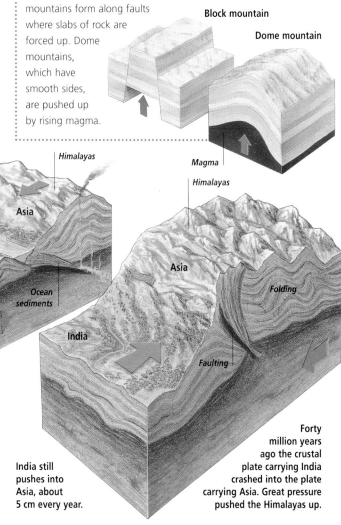

Block mountain

Dome mountain

Magma

Himalayas

Himalayas

Asia

Ocean sediments

Asia

Folding

India

Faulting

India still pushes into Asia, about 5 cm every year.

Forty million years ago the crustal plate carrying India crashed into the plate carrying Asia. Great pressure pushed the Himalayas up.

Glaciers

Glaciers are rivers of ice that form in mountain valleys and move slowly downhill. They have the power to carve spectacular landscapes, scouring the land with rocks they drag over its surface.

Features of a glacier

Most glaciers begin in hollows called cirques, high on mountain slopes. At the top, rock fragments fall into the glacier and are carried along in the ice. This rocky debris is called till. In steep areas the ice cracks into wedge-shaped crevasses. At the end of the glacier the ice melts and till is dumped on the ground.

As long as there is more snow falling at the top than ice melting at the end, a glacier continues to advance.

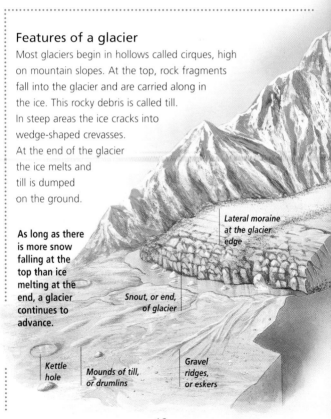

Lateral moraine at the glacier edge

Snout, or end, of glacier

Kettle hole

Mounds of till, or drumlins

Gravel ridges, or eskers

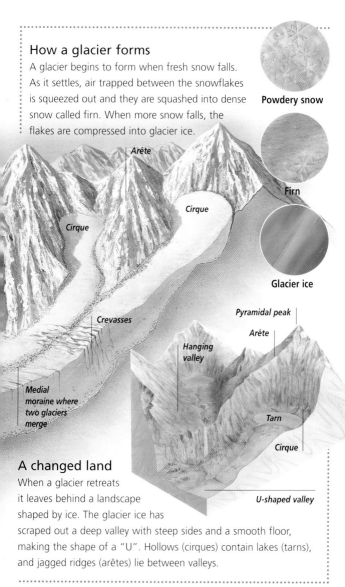

How a glacier forms

A glacier begins to form when fresh snow falls.
As it settles, air trapped between the snowflakes
is squeezed out and they are squashed into dense
snow called firn. When more snow falls, the
flakes are compressed into glacier ice.

Powdery snow

Firn

Glacier ice

Arête

Cirque

Cirque

Crevasses

Medial
moraine where
two glaciers
merge

Pyramidal peak

Arête

Hanging
valley

Tarn

Cirque

U-shaped valley

A changed land

When a glacier retreats
it leaves behind a landscape
shaped by ice. The glacier ice has
scraped out a deep valley with steep sides and a smooth floor,
making the shape of a "U". Hollows (cirques) contain lakes (tarns),
and jagged ridges (arêtes) lie between valleys.

Rivers – the upper course

Rivers are the highways of the natural world, carrying water downhill from mountains to the sea. They change the face of the land, carving long deep valleys and gorges through the rock.

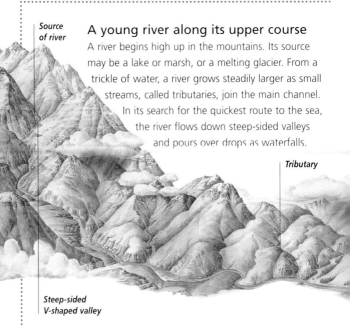

Source of river

A young river along its upper course

A river begins high up in the mountains. Its source may be a lake or marsh, or a melting glacier. From a trickle of water, a river grows steadily larger as small streams, called tributaries, join the main channel. In its search for the quickest route to the sea, the river flows down steep-sided valleys and pours over drops as waterfalls.

Tributary

Steep-sided V-shaped valley

Shaping the land

A river wears away the land by scratching and scraping the rocks and soil with the material it carries. This process is called abrasion. Small particles are dissolved in the water. Grains of sand or grit float in the water. Large rocks tumble along on the riverbed.

Waterfall and gorge formation

A waterfall is a cascade of water in a river that falls over the edge
of a cliff. It occurs where underlying soft rock has been worn away
by erosion to form a vertical drop. Where the water hits the
ground, the force is strong enough
to carve out a plunge pool.
As soft rock behind
the pool is eroded,
the waterfall recedes
(moves backwards),
leaving a steep-
sided gorge in
the rock.

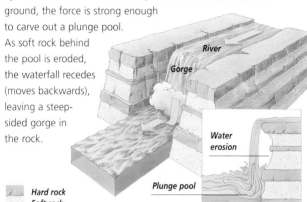

River

Gorge

Water
erosion

Plunge pool

Hard rock
Soft rock

Waterfall

Potholes

Potholes are hollows in the bedrock of rivers,
from a few centimetres to several metres across.
At the bottom are stones. Fast-flowing water
swirls them round, grinding
the pothole out of the rock
and, at the same time,
wearing the stones down.

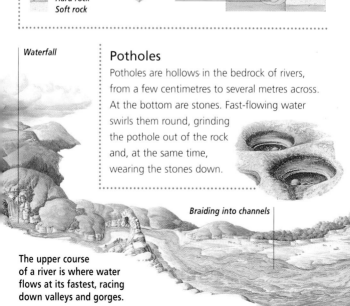

Braiding into channels

**The upper course
of a river is where water
flows at its fastest, racing
down valleys and gorges.**

Rivers – the lower course

A river reaches old age along its lower course, when it is in the last stage of its journey to the sea. It is often along this stretch that farmers grow crops and where towns and ports are built.

An old river along its lower course

As a river flows further away from its source, it carries more water and waterborne minerals, or sediment. The land levels off and the river cuts sideways into it, creating a wide, flat valley. This is the river's flood plain, where the soil is improved by the minerals left behind as the river floods over it. The river wanders slowly across its flood plain in large bends called meanders. Some bends are cut off to form oxbow lakes. When the river reaches the sea it drops the last of its sediment across a delta.

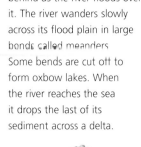

A flood plain is a low-lying area over which a river floods and deposits fertile sediment

The lower course of a river is where the flow of water slows and the channel widens as it crosses flatter land.

An oxbow lake is the remains of a meander

The fan-shaped delta at the end of the Colorado River, Mexico

Deltas at the coast

When a river slows as it reaches the sea, it drops the sediment, usually sand and silt, it has carried downstream. The sediment spreads out over a large area, called a delta. On the surface of a delta a river splits into a network of channels, called distributaries. A typical river delta at the coast has a triangular shape.

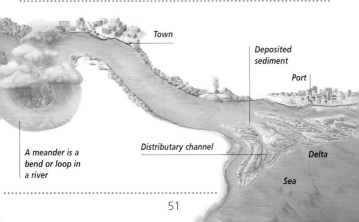

Town

Deposited sediment

Port

A meander is a bend or loop in a river

Distributary channel

Delta

Sea

Valleys

A valley is a long depression in the surface of the Earth. Valleys form where water and ice erode channels through mountains or in places where the Earth's crust cracks and the land falls away.

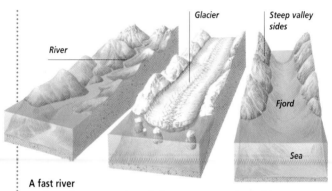

River

Glacier

Steep valley sides

Fjord

Sea

A fast river carries rocks downhill. They scour the river's bed, cutting a V-shaped valley.

As a glacier moves slowly downhill, rock pieces trapped in the ice scrape out a U-shaped valley.

In glacial areas a U-shaped valley that reaches the sea may become flooded to form a fjord.

Valleys formed by water and ice

A fast-moving river that flows down a steep mountain slope carves a deep V-shaped valley through the rock. If, in time, the valley is filled by a glacier, its sides will be worn steeper and its base will level off. It will become a U-shaped valley. In areas such as Norway and New Zealand, glaciers that once pushed their way to the sea have retreated and their long, narrow valleys have been drowned by seawater. These inlets are called fjords, from a Norwegian word.

Rift valley formation

A rift valley forms where a block of land slips down between two fault lines. For this to happen the faults must be roughly parallel to each other. The faults are at the edges of plates that are being pulled apart by movements of the Earth's crust. As the plates move away from each other, the land in between slowly subsides and a steep-sided rift valley forms.

The sunken block of land in a rift valley is called a graben.

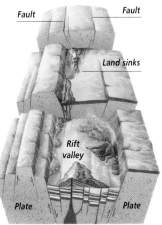

Fault

Fault

Land sinks

Rift valley

Plate

Plate

Canyon formation on land and at sea

A canyon is a narrow, steep-sided valley. On land a canyon is formed by the process of water erosion as a river wears its way downwards through rock. At sea, a submarine canyon is thought to have been eroded by the action of strong underwater currents.

The Grand Canyon, USA, is the result of erosion by the Colorado River.

Lakes

Lakes are bodies of water surrounded by land. The water can be fresh or salty. Most lakes are fed by rivers that flow into them. Rivers that flow from them take water out. Rain helps to keep lakes full.

Types of lakes

There are several different types of lakes, determined by how they were originally formed. An erosion lake forms when water collects in a hollow – either one gouged from the rock by a glacier or one scoured by the wind in a desert. A crater lake forms when rainwater collects at the top of an extinct volcano. When lava blocks a river, a lake "ponds up" behind it, such as the Sea of Galilee, Israel. Lakes also form in areas where the Earth's crust cracks open and water floods in.

Meander

Oxbow lake

An oxbow lake is formed where a river cuts through a U-shaped bend, or meander, leaving a curved lake behind.

Lake Rukwa

Lake Tanganyika

Lake Nyasa (Malawi)

Lake Baikal, Russia

At 1,637 metres deep, Lake Baikal is the world's deepest lake. It formed when the Earth's crust moved and split open. As rivers flowed into the rift, it filled with fresh water and the lake was formed. It is home to about 1,500 different species of animals and plants.

The transparent golomyanka fish live in Lake Baikal and nowhere else on Earth.

Lake Kivu   Lake Edward   Lake Albert   Lake Turkana

Lake Victoria

At 1,433 m deep, Lake Tanganyika is Africa's deepest lake.

Lakes in the Great Rift Valley, Africa

As the ground sank to form the Great Rift Valley, water filled the cracks on the valley floor to create lakes. Each one has a slightly different water composition, from fresh water to salty. There are no currents to circulate the water, and the lower depths contain lifeless "fossil" water millions of years old.

Caves

Caves are large hollows, formed as water eats away soft rock to leave tunnels and chambers. They are also made by the sea, by water running through glaciers and even inside flows of lava.

Inside a limestone cave system

A cave system in limestone rock can be an extensive network of interconnected wet and dry spaces, formed by the wearing action of water over thousands of years. The rise and fall of the water table means that different levels are eroded at different times.

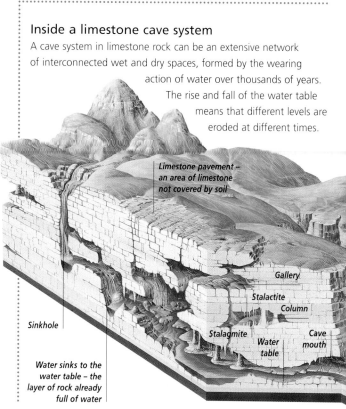

Limestone pavement – an area of limestone not covered by soil

Gallery

Stalactite

Column

Sinkhole

Stalagmite

Water table

Cave mouth

Water sinks to the water table – the layer of rock already full of water

How caves form

Most caves develop in sedimentary limestone rock. The soft rock is easily worn away. Rainwater, which is acidic, sinks through holes into cracks in the rock. It dissolves the rock to form chambers and passages. As the water drains away, the cave fills with air above the water table.

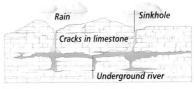

Rainwater contains acids that dissolve the calcium carbonate that forms limestone.

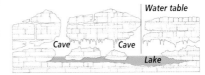

Caves are hollowed out as water flows along lines of weakness in the limestone.

Where water cannot sink through hard rock (an impermeable layer), it forms a river

Stalagmites and stalactites form columns if they touch.

Stalagmites and stalactites

Water dripping in a limestone cave leaves behind tiny amounts of a mineral called calcite. It hardens into rock. Calcite "icicles", called stalactites, cling tightly to the roof of a cave, while calcite spikes, called stalagmites, grow upwards from the floor.

Sand deserts

A desert is a dry area where very little rain falls. High winds, extremes of temperature – hot in the day and cold at night – and occasional rushes of fast-flowing water create a distinctive landscape.

A desert landscape

The landscape of a typical sand desert contains many distinctive features. Deep channels, called wadis, mark out watercourses. Dry for much of the year, wadis fill with water after heavy rain. Hills, called mesas and buttes, rise up from the desert floor, as do piles of sand called dunes. Windblown sand erodes hard rock into arches and columns.

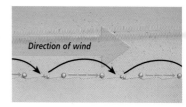

Direction of wind

Wind blows small sand grains along in a series of short hops. As the grains land, they knock large grains forwards.

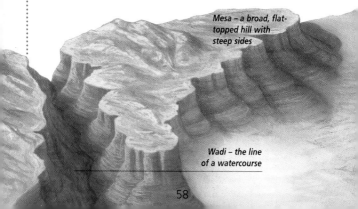

Mesa – a broad, flat-topped hill with steep sides

Wadi – the line of a watercourse

The four main types of sand dunes

Barchan dunes are crescent-shaped. They form where the wind blows from the same direction. Seif dunes are steep-sided ridges, formed where the winds blow at right angles to one another. Star dunes form where the wind blows from all directions. Transverse dunes form at right angles to the wind.

Sand dunes vary in size. The highest rise up to 200 m from the desert floor.

Butte – a smaller version of a mesa

Seif dune

Pedestal rock

Eroded arch

Mushroom rock

Direction of wind

Barchan dune

Transverse dune

Star dune

Hamada – a bare, rocky pavement

Oasis

A desert's sand comes from the bedrock that forms its floor. Wind and water action erode the rock, wearing it down into tiny particles, or grains.

Deserts and oases

Almost one-third of the Earth's land surface is covered in deserts of one kind or another, from the sandy expanses of Africa and Asia to the icy wastes of Antarctica. Life adapts to the harsh conditions.

How an oasis forms

In some deserts fresh water comes to the surface to form a wet area called an oasis (plural: oases). The water often comes from rain that falls on distant mountains. It travels underground through rocks that hold water. An oasis forms in a hollow that dips below the top of the water table. Water leaves the rock and fills the hollow.

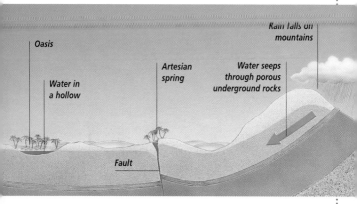

Oasis

Rain falls on mountains

Water in a hollow

Artesian spring

Water seeps through porous underground rocks

Fault

Life at an oasis

An oasis is a desert's watering hole. Animals gather to drink its water and people often settle nearby. Plants, such as date palm trees, grow at an oasis, providing shade and energy-rich fruit.

Hot and cold deserts

Some deserts, such as the Sahara in Africa, are hot deserts, where high temperatures are felt during the day. Others, such as Taklimakan in China, are cold deserts with low daytime temperatures. Even the frozen continent of Antarctica has deserts, called polar deserts.

The Gobi is a cold desert in Asia, where winter temperatures are low.

Cacti – plants of the desert

Because it is hard for desert plants to find enough water to live, they have adapted to the very dry arid conditions. One group of plants, called cacti, have long roots which seek out water from deep underground. They store water in their thick swollen stems. Ridges on the stems allow cacti to swell up as they draw water inside themselves.

The saguaro cactus grows in Mexico's Sonoran Desert. It can grow 15 m tall and live for more than 200 years.

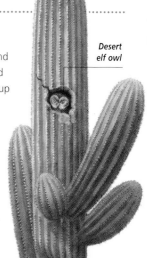

Desert elf owl

61

Volcanoes

A volcano is a hole, or vent, in the Earth's crust from which molten rock, ash and gas escape. Volcanoes often occur at weak spots in the crust, especially along the boundaries of the Earth's plates.

A volcano erupts

A volcano erupts when molten rock, called magma, rises up from the Earth's mantle. It comes to the surface through a vent in the crust. Magma that reaches the surface is called lava. Rough-skinned lava is called a'a, and smooth-skinned lava is called pahoehoe. Lava from underwater volcanoes is called pillow lava.

Crater

Side vent

Lava flow

Old magma chamber

New magma chamber

Lava can reach 1,200°C, yet it only takes 5 or 10 minutes after pahoehoe lava (right) has stopped flowing before its surface cools down and sets hard.

Types of volcanoes

A composite volcano is tall and steep-sided. It has frequent lava eruptions. A cinder cone volcano is flatter and throws out gas and ash. A shield volcano has several openings, or vents, out of which lava flows. A fissure volcano occurs along a crack in the Earth's crust, letting lava out over a long distance, usually under the sea.

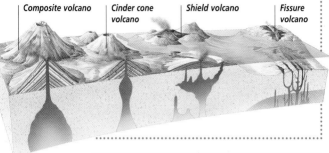

Composite volcano *Cinder cone volcano* *Shield volcano* *Fissure volcano*

After the eruption of Mount Pinatubo in the Philippines in 1991, volcanic ash rained down on the people who lived nearby.

Material thrown out by a volcano

The solid products ejected by a volcano are called pyroclasts. They include ash (tiny particles); lapilli (small pebbles); blocks (large chunks of rock); bombs (large blobs of molten lava); and pumice and cinder (lightweight rocks full of gas bubbles). Poisonous gases are also given off, especially sulphur dioxide and carbon dioxide.

Volcanic landscape

The landscape around a volcano covers a large area of land. The soil is fertile and is good for agriculture. Under the ground there is hot water, which can be used to provide a source of power.

Volcanoes in the landscape

A volcano that is erupting, or that has recently erupted, is called active. One that is not erupting, but that may do so again in the future, is dormant and one that will probably never erupt again is extinct. No matter what state a volcano is in, the landscape it created will contain a range of special features both above and below the ground.

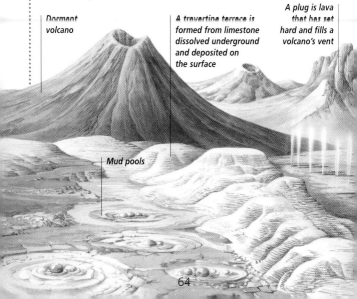

Dormant volcano

A travertine terrace is formed from limestone dissolved underground and deposited on the surface

A plug is lava that has set hard and fills a volcano's vent

Mud pools

Hot water features

Hot water makes several distinctive features in a volcanic landscape. A geyser is a fountain of hot water that squirts into the sky through a hole in the ground. A fumarole is an opening that releases jets of hot steam and other gases. Springs bubble with hot water, and if this is mixed with ash and other particles they become mud pools. The minerals they deposit harden to form rocky terraces.

A geyser forces hot water and steam into the air, sometimes at regular intervals.

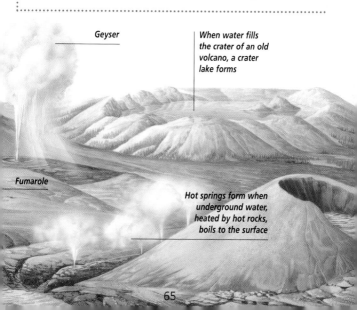

Geyser

When water fills the crater of an old volcano, a crater lake forms

Fumarole

Hot springs form when underground water, heated by hot rocks, boils to the surface

Earthquakes

An earthquake is a shaking of the ground. It is caused by a release of energy as rocks move under the ground. Damage is caused when the shaking reaches the surface.

Fault line movements

As the Earth's plates move against each other, they make cracks, or faults, along lines of weakness in the crust. In a normal fault, a block of rock slips down as the crust is pulled apart. In a reverse fault, a block of rock is pushed above another as the crust is squeezed. In a tear fault, blocks of rock slide past each other in opposite directions.

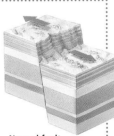

Normal fault

Tear fault

Reverse fault

Vibrations from an earthquake

The shakes from an earthquake begin under the ground at a point called the focus. Vibrations move out from the focus in concentric circles, like ripples across water. Most damage occurs at the epicentre, which is the point on the surface directly above the focus.

An earthquake in Kobe, Japan, in 1995 brought chaos to the city's roads.

Earthquake damage

An earthquake on land causes buildings to fall and can start fires. Landslides and avalanches bury all in their path. An earthquake under the seabed causes seismic sea waves, or tsunamis. They smash into the coast and wash far inland.

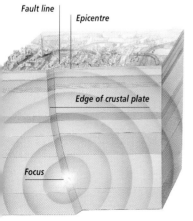

Fault line

Epicentre

Edge of crustal plate

Focus

Wave patterns

An earthquake sends out shock, or seismic, waves. Body waves, called primary waves and secondary waves, travel inside the Earth. P-waves are fast. S-waves are slow. Surface waves, called Love waves and Rayleigh waves, move quickly across the surface.

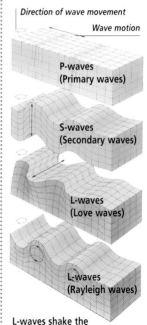

Direction of wave movement

Wave motion

P-waves (Primary waves)

S-waves (Secondary waves)

L-waves (Love waves)

L-waves (Rayleigh waves)

L-waves shake the ground from side to side and up and down. They cause the most damage.

Weather and climate

....

Climate zones 70

Winds 72

Fronts and air masses 74

Clouds and precipitation 76

Storms 78

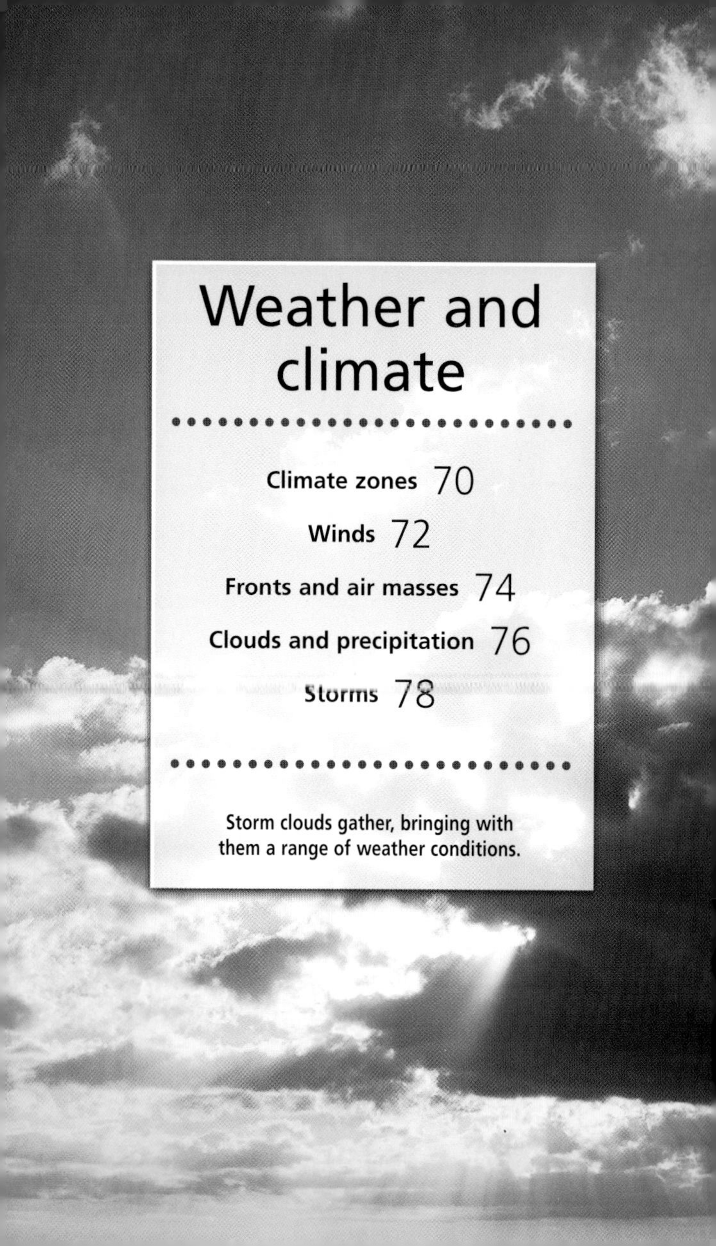

....

Storm clouds gather, bringing with
them a range of weather conditions.

Climate zones

**Heat from the Sun makes air and water
move around the Earth. It causes the weather.
The typical weather pattern of an area over
a long period of time is called the climate.**

Earth's climate zones

There are three main climate zones, according to how far they
are from the equator. They are the hot tropics near the equator,
the cold polar regions and the warm temperate areas in between.
As well as being hot, the tropics are also wet because the warm
air rises and cools, forming clouds and rain. At the poles the snow
and ice reflect most of the Sun's heat, making them colder still.
The temperate regions have warm summers, cold winters and rain
all year round. Each zone has its own typical plants and animals.

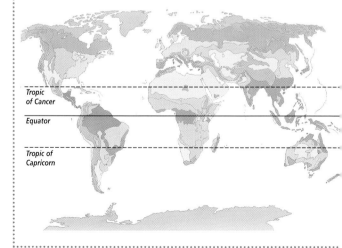

Tropic
of Cancer

Equator

Tropic of
Capricorn

Rays from the Sun

Because the Earth is round, the tropics are heated more than the poles. The Sun's rays hit the tropics full on and make this a hot region. Near the poles the rays strike at a low angle and spread out, making cold regions. The regions in between are warm.

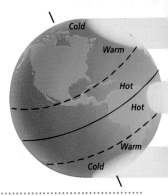

Cold
Warm
Hot
Hot
Warm
Cold

Polar and tundra
Cold and dry all year

Cold forest
Cold winter, warm summer

Mountain
Snow higher up, warm and wet lower down

Temperate
Mild and rainy all year

Mediterranean
Mild winter, warm summer

Dry grassland
Hot, dry summer, snowy winter

Desert
Dry all year

Tropical grassland
Hot all year, wet and dry seasons

Tropical rainforest
Hot and wet all year

Winds

Wind is air moving from one place to another. Air moves from warm areas to cool ones, which is why warm air rises at the equator and moves towards the poles. Cold air moves the other way.

Winds and air pressure

The weight of air above ground produces a force that presses down. The force is called air pressure. Warm air rises because it is "lighter" than cold air. It spreads out, so the air particles are further apart, creating an area of low air pressure. Cool air is "heavier" because the air particles are closer together. It sinks to the ground to produce an area of high air pressure. Surface winds occur when air moves from an area of high pressure to an area of low pressure.

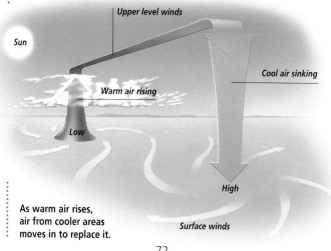

Sun

Upper level winds

Cool air sinking

Warm air rising

Low

High

As warm air rises, air from cooler areas moves in to replace it.

Surface winds

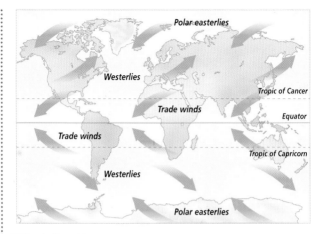

Wind directions

Winds fall into three belts, depending on the direction in which they blow. The wind patterns in the two hemispheres are mirror images of each other. In the tropics, winds that blow towards the equator are called trade winds. Polar easterlies are cold winds that blow out from the poles. Westerlies blow in the temperate regions.

Land and sea breezes

During the day land warms faster than sea. As warm air rises above the land, cool air blows in from the sea. This is a sea breeze. At night the air flows change direction because sea stays warmer longer than land. Air flows out to sea. This is a land breeze.

Day

Breeze blows from sea to land

Land   Sea

Night

Breeze blows from land to sea

Land   Sea

Fronts and air masses

When a body, or mass, of air is moved out of the way by another, the weather changes along the boundary, or front, between them.

Warm and cold fronts

When a mass of cold air meets a mass of warm air, the two do not simply mix together. Instead, a boundary, called a front, remains between them. It separates air masses of different temperature. Where one air mass meets another, stormy, changeable weather occurs at the fronts. A warm front is where warm air moves in to an area and replaces cold air. A cold front is where cold air moves in and replaces warm air.

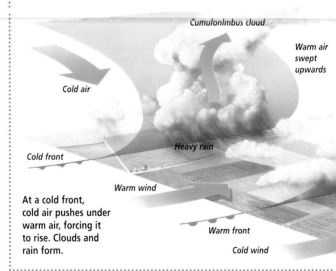

Cumulonimbus cloud

Warm air swept upwards

Cold air

Heavy rain

Cold front

Warm wind

At a cold front, cold air pushes under warm air, forcing it to rise. Clouds and rain form.

Warm front

Cold wind

Air masses

An air mass is a body of air close to the surface of the Earth. It may stay in one area for days or even weeks, before being moved on by winds. Air masses are classified according to the area where they began, called their source. Most air masses begin either in the tropics or at the poles.

A tropical maritime air mass develops over warm seas (above top).
A polar continental air mass develops over land near the poles (above).

Occluded front

A cold front moves towards a warm front and may join up with it. If this happens the cold air pushes the warm air up and an occluded front occurs. It brings storm clouds and heavy rain.

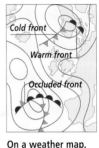

Cold front

Warm front

Occluded front

On a weather map, different symbols are used to show cold, warm and occluded fronts.

Warm air rises

At a warm front, warm air rises above cold air. As it rises, the water vapour in the warm air cools and condenses to form clouds and rain.

Rain

Cold air

Direction of front's movement

Clouds and precipitation

A cloud is a mass of water droplets or ice crystals in the air. Water is always present in the air, as a gas called water vapour. It changes into water droplets or ice crystals. They fall as rain and snow.

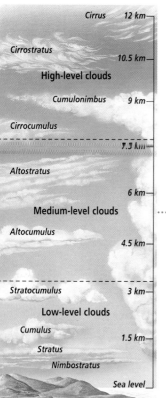

Cirrus 12 km

Cirrostratus 10.5 km

High-level clouds

Cumulonimbus 9 km

Cirrocumulus

7.5 km

Altostratus

6 km

Medium-level clouds

Altocumulus

4.5 km

Stratocumulus 3 km

Low-level clouds

Cumulus

1.5 km

Stratus

Nimbostratus

Sea level

Cloud types

Clouds fall into three families: cirrus (meaning curl of hair), cumulus (meaning heap) and stratus (meaning layer). They are made of ice or water according to their height in the sky. High-level clouds are made of ice crystals. Medium-level clouds are made of water droplets and ice crystals. Low-level clouds are made just of water droplets.

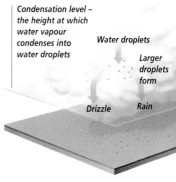

Condensation level – the height at which water vapour condenses into water droplets

Water droplets

Larger droplets form

Drizzle   Rain

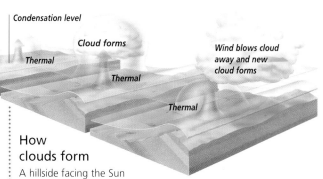

Condensation level

Cloud forms

Thermal

Wind blows cloud away and new cloud forms

Thermal

Thermal

How clouds form

A hillside facing the Sun heats up more than nearby land. A large bubble of air, called a thermal, rises. As it rises, air inside the thermal cools. Water vapour changes, or condenses, into water droplets and a cloud forms. As wind blows the cloud away, a new cloud forms in its place.

The types of precipitation depend on whether a cloud carries ice crystals, water droplets or both.

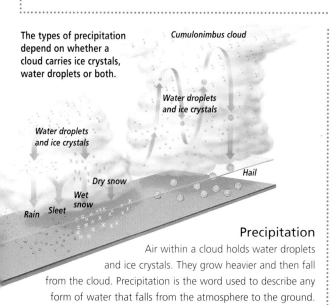

Cumulonimbus cloud

Water droplets and ice crystals

Water droplets and ice crystals

Hail

Dry snow

Wet snow

Rain   Sleet

Precipitation

Air within a cloud holds water droplets and ice crystals. They grow heavier and then fall from the cloud. Precipitation is the word used to describe any form of water that falls from the atmosphere to the ground. It can fall as a liquid, such as rain, or as a solid, such as snow.

Storms

Storms are times of bad weather, linked to the growth of strong winds and huge clouds. One type of storm brings bright sparks of lightning and the booming sound of thunder.

Inside a thundercloud

Thunder and lightning occur when there is a build-up of different electrical charges inside a storm cloud. Strong air currents inside the cloud make ice and water particles bump together, creating a charge of static electricity which, when released, is seen as lightning.

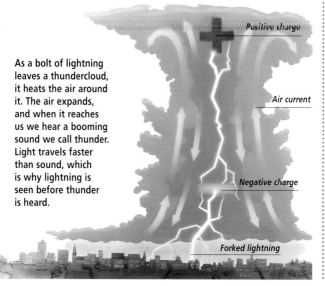

As a bolt of lightning leaves a thundercloud, it heats the air around it. The air expands, and when it reaches us we hear a booming sound we call thunder. Light travels faster than sound, which is why lightning is seen before thunder is heard.

Positive charge

Air current

Negative charge

Forked lightning

78

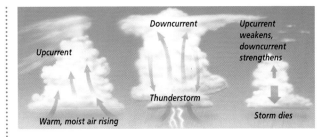

Upcurrent

Downcurrent

Upcurrent weakens, downcurrent strengthens

Thunderstorm

Warm, moist air rising

Storm dies

How a thunderstorm forms, then dies away

A thunderstorm forms from a small cumulus cloud when there is a rising upcurrent of warm, moist air. Precipitation falls, pulling air down to create a downcurrent. The clash of air currents sets off a thunderstorm. It dies out when the upcurrent weakens.

Types of lightning

Lightning is a giant spark of electricity that jumps from a cloud. There are several types of lightning. Lightning that jumps inside clouds is called sheet lightning. If it leaves the cloud and strikes the ground, then it is forked lightning. Ball lightning is still something of a mystery. It appears suddenly as a sphere and floats through the air. It is sometimes seen inside buildings and aircraft.

A bolt of forked lightning like this super-heats a narrow column of air (about 5 cm wide) to 30,000°C in an instant.

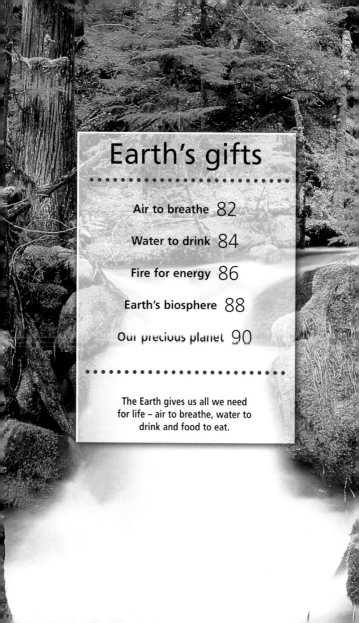

Earth's gifts

Air to breathe 82

Water to drink 84

Fire for energy 86

Earth's biosphere 88

Our precious planet 90

The Earth gives us all we need for life – air to breathe, water to drink and food to eat.

Air to breathe

Our lungs take in oxygen gas and give out carbon dioxide gas. Green leaves take in carbon dioxide and give out oxygen. In this way the air we breathe is constantly recycled.

The oxygen cycle

Oxygen is one of the gases in the Earth's atmosphere. Living things need it to survive. The process that puts oxygen into the atmosphere, and also takes it away, is called the oxygen cycle. Animals breathe in oxygen. This is called respiration. In the daytime, green plants put oxygen back into the atmosphere. This is called photosynthesis. The oxygen cycle never stops.

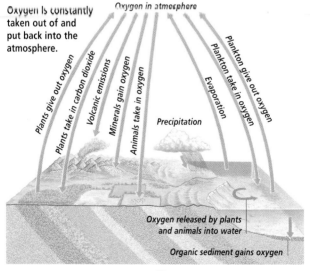

Oxygen is constantly taken out of and put back into the atmosphere.

Oxygen in atmosphere

Plants give out oxygen

Plants take in carbon dioxide

Volcanic emissions

Minerals gain oxygen

Animals take in oxygen

Precipitation

Evaporation

Plankton take in oxygen

Plankton give out oxygen

Oxygen released by plants and animals into water

Organic sediment gains oxygen

Rainforests, like this one in Colombia, are areas of dense tropical forests.

How rainforests make oxygen

Rainforests contain evergreen trees and a great variety of other plants. They occur where temperatures are high and rainfall is heavy – at least 200 centimetres per year – but are shrinking fast due to pollution and the cutting down of the forests by people. The green leaves of the forest use sunlight to change carbon dioxide in the air into their food. During this process (known as photosynthesis) oxygen gas is released from the leaves into the atmosphere.

Today rainforests (green) cover less than 10 per cent of the Earth's land.

Water to drink

All living things need water to survive. It falls from the sky, fills rivers and lakes, and drains into the sea. After it has been cleaned it is safe for people to drink.

The water cycle

The Sun heats water on the Earth's surface and changes it into an invisible gas called water vapour. This change is called evaporation. The water vapour gas rises. Higher up in the atmosphere the air is cooler and the gas changes back into drops of liquid water. This is called condensation. The condensed water forms clouds. When water falls from the clouds it returns to the Earth's surface and completes the water cycle. The amount of water on the Earth stays the same because it is constantly recycled.

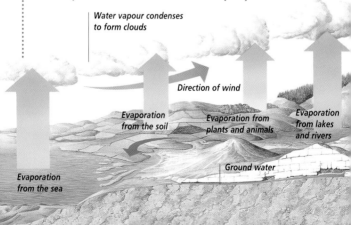

Water vapour condenses to form clouds

Direction of wind

Evaporation from the soil

Evaporation from plants and animals

Evaporation from lakes and rivers

Evaporation from the sea

Ground water

Water for drinking

Water for drinking comes from several sources, such as lakes and reservoirs, rivers and wells. From here it is sent along pipes and aqueducts to water treatment plants where it is filtered through layers of gravel and sand. As water seeps through the filter beds, impurities are removed. It is then clean and safe to drink.

A treatment plant cleans water, making it ready to drink.

Because of air currents and weather patterns, water that evaporates in one place falls as rain far away.

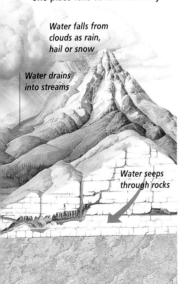

Water falls from clouds as rain, hail or snow

Water drains into streams

Water seeps through rocks

Seawater

Seawater contains many different minerals. The two most abundant are sodium and chlorine, which together form common salt. On average, 1 litre of seawater contains 30 grams of salt. A process called desalination removes salt from seawater to produce fresh water to drink.

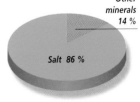

Other minerals 14 %

Salt 86 %

Salt is the largest mineral component of seawater.

Fire for energy

Coal, oil and natural gas are called fossil fuels because they come from the changed remains of ancient plants and animals. They are important sources of energy, giving light and heat.

Dead vegetation forms peat | *Peat transformed into lignite* | *Bituminous coal forms under pressure* | *Anthracite coal seam finally forms*

Coal formation

Coal is a black mineral substance formed from the remains of ancient vegetation. As plants died, they sank into swamps where an absence of oxygen meant they did not rot. Instead, they turned into a fibrous substance called peat. As the layers of peat were pressed together they turned into lignite. More pressure turned the lignite into bituminous coal, which in turn sometimes changed into anthracite coal. Both types of coal are mined.

Oil and gas formation

Oil and natural gas formed millions of years ago at the bottom of the sea. When tiny sea-living organisms died, they drifted to the seabed, where they were covered by sediments which set into rock. Under great pressure, the partly decayed material was squeezed and was turned into oil and gas. Both moved slowly upwards and collected in large pools. It is these pools that drilling rigs drill in to.

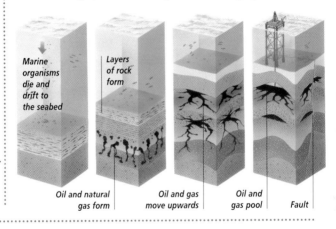

Marine organisms die and drift to the seabed

Layers of rock form

Oil and natural gas form

Oil and gas move upwards

Oil and gas pool

Fault

Extraction of coal, oil and gas

Fossil fuels are extracted by drilling and mining. Most coal is mined on land. Deep coal is extracted by digging vertical tunnels called shafts. Surface coal is reached by horizontal tunnels called drifts, or by digging the top layers away until the coal is reached. Oil and gas are extracted by drilling for them on land and at sea.

A drilling rig such as this is fixed to the seabed, where it drills for oil and gas.

Earth's biosphere

Life on Earth exists in the sky, on the land and in the sea. Each one provides a different habitat. Together, all these habitats form Earth's biosphere.

Ecosystems

Ecosystems are units of the biosphere. They are communities of living things – all animals and plants – and their environment. They range from ponds to forests.

A rainforest and all the species of animals and plants within it are an ecosystem.

Habitats and niches

Habitats and niches are smaller units of the Earth's biosphere. Habitats are the natural places where plants and animals live. For example, caves, lakes, mountains, forests and oceans are all types of habitats. Within habitats there are niches. A niche is the position that a living thing occupies within an ecosystem. It is the individual home of a plant or an animal, together with the way in which it leads its life.

Within a rainforest ecosystem, different species of plants and animals share the same habitats.

A biosphere experiment

In the Biosphere Project of the early 1990s, seven ecosystems, including a mini rainforest, ocean and desert, were built inside a massive airtight glasshouse. Eight scientists lived there for two years, closely studying the Earth's natural living systems, how they interact with one another and how they are affected by humans.

The rainforest ecosystem created for the Biosphere Project, USA.

Our precious planet

Today's humans have interfered with the Earth's delicate environment. The temperature is rising and the air is filling with deadly fumes. Ways are now being found to protect Earth for the future.

Pollution harms the planet

Pollution is anything that damages the environment. Smoke and exhaust fumes that enter the atmosphere, chemicals released into the oceans and rivers, and pesticides sprayed on to the land are all forms of pollution. Poisonous gases are released when oil and coal are burned. They pollute the air and, by mixing with water vapour, they become part of the water cycle. Water droplets form that contain harmful acids. The droplets fall to ground as acid rain, which damages soil, poisons lakes, rots stone and kills plants and trees.

Oil spilled at sea pollutes the oceans and harms wildlife. It floats on the water's surface and sticks to seabirds' feathers.

Global warming

During the 20th century the Earth's temperature rose by a fraction of a degree each year. This is called global warming. It is caused by the build-up of gases in the atmosphere. They encircle the planet and are called greenhouse gases since they are ones that stop heat from escaping. They reflect heat back to the Earth. The temperature rises, the oceans warm and ice melts at the poles.

Greenhouse gases come from aerosols and old refrigerators.

Greenhouse gases come from burning forests and fossil fuels.

Sunlight

Some heat escapes into space

Sunlight reflected off clouds

Heat trapped by greenhouse gases

Greenhouse gases come from car exhausts and fertilisers.

Heat reflected back by clouds

Sunlight reflected off Earth's surface

Heat from the Earth

Greenhouse gases trap heat, causing the Earth's temperature to rise.

Greenhouse gases come from animals' digestion, swamps, rotting vegetation and refuse, and gas pipes.

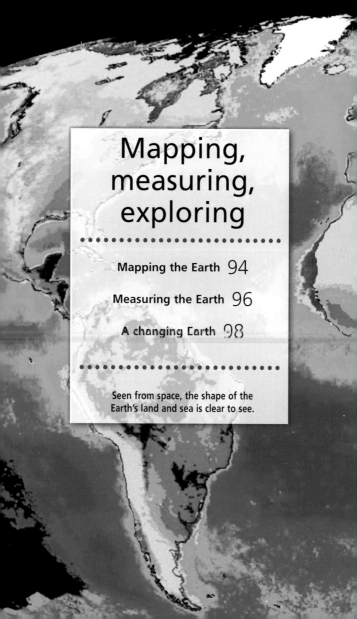

Mapping, measuring, exploring

Mapping the Earth 94

Measuring the Earth 96

A changing Earth 98

Seen from space, the shape of the Earth's land and sea is clear to see.

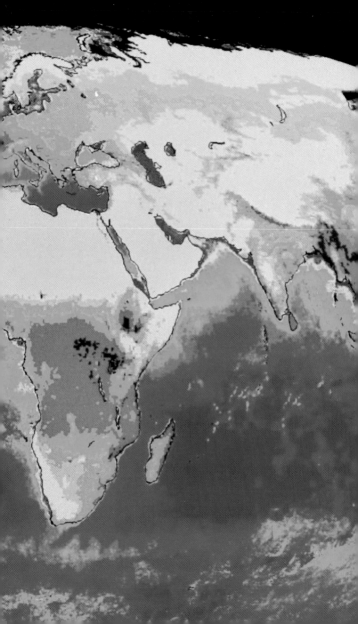

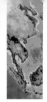

Mapping the Earth

Maps help us to record information about the Earth, including the size and shape of the oceans and continents, right down to the smallest hills.

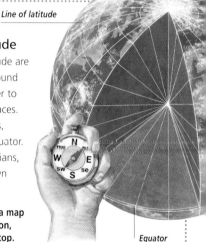

Line of longitude

Line of latitude

Latitude and longitude

Lines of latitude and longitude are a grid of imaginary lines around the globe that make it easier to draw maps and pinpoint places. Lines of latitude, or parallels, are circles parallel to the equator. Lines of longitude, or meridians, are lines drawn up and down from pole to pole.

A compass points a map in the right direction, with north at the top.

Equator

A cylindrical projection is made as if the Earth has been wrapped in a tube of paper.

Map projections

A projection is the way in which map-makers show the curved surface of the Earth on a flat map. No projection is perfect, since they all distort, or change, the true shape and size of the land and sea.

94

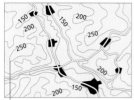
Contour

A contour map uses lines to show the height of the land.

Different types of maps

Imaginary lines, called contours, are a way of showing the rise and fall of the land on a map. They show all the places that are the same height above sea level. On a geological map, colours are used to show the extent and location of different types of material, such as sand, clay, chalk, limestone and granite.

☐ Alluvial deposits
☐ Sandy clay   ☐ Limestone
☐ Clay   ☐ Granite

A geological map uses colours.

Use of false-colour photography

Satellite images of the Earth can be displayed in colours that are not true-to-life. This technique, called false-colour photography, is useful for mapping specific types of information.

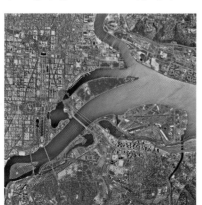

For example, images taken over a desert area can be used to reveal how far and how fast the desert is spreading.

False-colour image of Washington, DC, USA. It reveals "hot" areas where lots of energy is released, shown in pink and red.

Measuring the Earth

The Earth is measured every minute of every day. Machines on land, at sea, in the sky and under the ground measure the planet's ever-changing conditions.

Measuring the weather

Official observers in all countries record surface weather conditions at agreed times each day. They use the same types of instruments to measure temperature, rainfall, air pressure, wind speed, amount of sunshine and humidity. At the poles, and in deserts and dense forests, automatic weather stations have been set up to collect and transmit similar information.

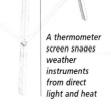

A thermometer screen shades weather instruments from direct light and heat

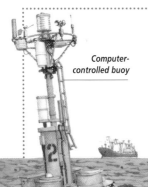

Computer-controlled buoy

Weather buoys at sea

A buoy is a floating platform fixed to the seabed. A weather buoy collects information about wind speed, wave height and sea and air temperature. The information is then sent to ships and weather stations.

Weather balloons

What happens high up in the atmosphere affects the weather near the Earth's surface. To obtain temperature, air pressure and humidity measurements, gas-filled weather balloons rise into the sky. They carry recording instruments, called radiosondes, which send signals back to weather stations on the ground.

It takes an hour for a weather balloon to rise 20 km.

Radiosonde

Seismographs detect earthquake vibrations and record them on paper (below).

Measuring earthquakes

A seismograph is used to record and measure earthquakes. As the ground shakes, the instrument detects vibrations moving through the ground and records them on paper or a computer. The record made by a seismograph is called a seismogram, from which the size and location of an earthquake can be calculated.

A changing Earth

Our knowledge of the Earth is still growing. As new ways are found of exploring the planet, new facts are discovered. Some tell us about the Earth today. Others reveal what it was like long ago.

Satellite exploration

Satellites that travel around the Earth take photographs which help us to see the Earth in a new way. The outlines of continents and the location of mountain ranges, rivers and lakes can be clearly seen. From these images, accurate maps can be created which show the exact shapes of the Earth's land and sea. Some satellites watch the weather, recording how it changes from day to day.

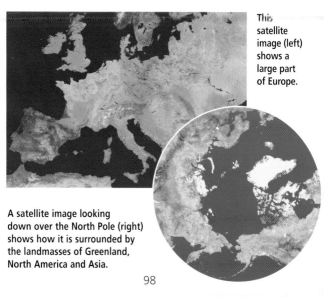

This satellite image (left) shows a large part of Europe.

A satellite image looking down over the North Pole (right) shows how it is surrounded by the landmasses of Greenland, North America and Asia.

Ice reveals the past

The history of the Earth's climate over several thousand years is trapped in the ice sheet of Antarctica. The snow that falls there contains facts about the year in which it fell. By examining ice cores taken from deep inside the ice it is possible to tell when warm and cool years occurred.

Volcanic dust found in ice reveals how often volcanoes erupted.

Deep sea exploration

Scientists are now discovering more of the Earth's secrets by exploring the seabed. Manned and unmanned diving vehicles search for mineral deposits, as well as mapping ocean trenches and other deep sea features. They are also finding new forms of life which can survive at great depths in total darkness.

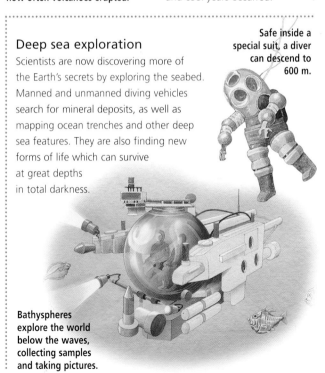

Safe inside a special suit, a diver can descend to 600 m.

Bathyspheres explore the world below the waves, collecting samples and taking pictures.

Fact file

The Earth is a planet of amazing facts – from
the highest mountain to the deepest sea trench,
the calmest breeze to the strongest hurricane.

Earth facts

Use this section to look up facts about the Earth.
The information is presented in a series of tables
which contain facts about the Earth's land,
sky and sea.

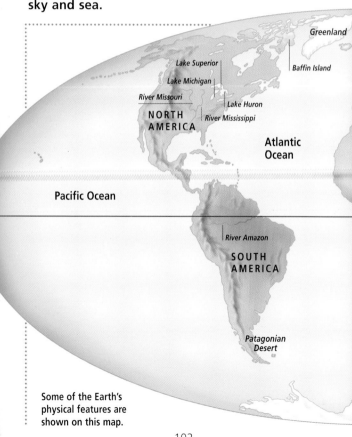

Greenland

Baffin Island

Lake Superior

Lake Michigan

River Missouri

NORTH
AMERICA

Lake Huron

River Mississippi

Atlantic
Ocean

Pacific Ocean

River Amazon

SOUTH
AMERICA

Patagonian
Desert

Some of the Earth's
physical features are
shown on this map.

Land accounts for about 29 per cent of the total surface area of the Earth – the other 71 per cent is water. The total area covered by land is about 149 million sq km. The total area covered by water is about 360 million sq km.

Land

Sea

Arctic Ocean

River Yenisey

River Angara

River Volga

Lake Baikal

EUROPE

Caspian Sea

River Selenga

ASIA

Gobi Desert

River Huang He

River Chang Jiang

Mt Everest

Sahara Desert

Arabian Desert

Pacific Ocean

AFRICA

River Nile

Borneo

Lake Victoria

Indian Ocean

New Guinea

Madagascar

AUSTRALASIA

Australian Desert

River Darling

River Murray

ANTARCTICA

The ice covered continent of Antarctica is the least populated region on the Earth. It is a place of great natural beauty, and is protected by international agreements.

CONTINENTS

Continent	Area	% of total	Highest point
Asia	44,493,000 sq km	29.5	Mt Everest 8,848 m
Africa	30,293,000 sq km	20.2	Kilimanjaro 5,895 m
N America	24,454,000 sq km	16.3	Mt McKinley 6,194 m
S America	17,838,000 sq km	11.9	Aconcagua 6,959 m
Antarctica	13,975,000 sq km	9.3	Vinson Massif 5,140 m
Europe	10,245,000 sq km	6.8	Elbrus 5,642 m
Australasia	8,945,000 sq km	6	Puncak Jaya 5,030 m

Until Mt Everest's height was measured in 1852, it was known to surveyors as Peak XV. It was named Everest after Sir George Everest, the Surveyor General of India.

EARTH'S HIGHEST MOUNTAINS

Mountain	Mountain range	Height
Everest	Himalayas	8,848 m
K2 (Mt Godwin-Austen)	Himalayas	8,611 m
Kangchenjunga	Himalayas	8,598 m
Lhotse	Himalayas	8,501 m
Makalu I	Himalayas	8,470 m

EARTH'S LONGEST GLACIERS

Glacier	Location	Length
Lambert-Fisher	Antarctica	515 km
Novaya Zemlya	Russia	418 km
Arctic Institute	Antarctica	362 km
Nimrod-Lennox-King	Antarctica	290 km
Denman	Antarctica	241 km

Cactus plants grow in dry
areas, such as deserts.
Their flowers are often
large and colourful.

EARTH'S LARGEST DESERTS

Desert	Location	Area
Sahara	North Africa	9,000,000 sq km
Arabian	Asia	2,330,000 sq km
Gobi	Asia	1,166,000 sq km
Patagonian	South America	673,000 sq km
Australian	Australia	647,000 sq km

EARTH'S DEEPEST CAVES

Cave	Country	Depth
Lamprechtsofen-Vogelshacht	Austria	1,632 m
Gouffre Mirolda (Lucien Bouclier)	France	1,610 m
Réseau Jean Bernard	France	1,602 m
Shakta Vjacheslav Pantjukhina	Georgia	1,508 m
Sistema Huautla	Mexico	1,475 m

Volcanic eruptions are measured using the Volcanic Explosivity Index, or VEI. Eruptions are graded from 0 to 8, determined by how much ash is ejected. There are about two VEI 8 eruptions every 100,000 years. Only four eruptions in the last 10,000 years have been classed with a VEI of 7.

VOLCANIC EXPLOSIVITY INDEX

VEI	Description	Ash height	Amount of ash ejected
0	Non-explosive	Below 100 m	Thousands of cubic metres
1	Gentle	100–1,000 m	Tens of thousands of cubic metres
2	Explosive	1–5 km	Millions of cubic metres
3	Severe	3–15 km	Tens of millions of cubic metres
4	Cataclysmic	10–25 km	Hundreds of millions of cubic metres
5	Paroxysmal	Above 25 km	One cubic kilometre
6	Colossal	Above 25 km	Tens of cubic kilometres
7	Super-colossal	Above 25 km	Hundreds of cubic kilometres
8	Mega-colossal	Above 25 km	Thousands of cubic kilometres

MAJOR VOLCANIC ERUPTIONS

Volcano and country	Eruption	VEI
Tambora, Indonesia	1815	7
Santorini, Greece	around 1470 BC	6
Krakatau, Indonesia	1883	6
Santa Maria, Guatemala	1902	6
Mount St. Helens, USA	1980	5
Pinatubo, Philippines	1991	5

MERCALLI EARTHQUAKE INTENSITY SCALE

Level	Characteristics
1	Not felt
2	Felt by few people
3	Felt by few people, mostly indoors; objects swing if suspended
4	Felt by many people indoors; windows and doors rattle
5	Felt by nearly everyone; small objects fall; doors move
6	Felt by everyone; furniture moves; windows break; trees shake
7	Difficult to stand; minor building damage; small landslides
8	Difficult to steer cars; chimneys fall; tree branches break
9	General panic; ground cracks; underground pipes break
10	Buildings collapse; rivers flood
11	Most buildings damaged; bridges fall
12	Almost total destruction; large rock masses move

The Mercalli Earthquake Intensity Scale is useful where readings from earthquake recorders are not available. The Richter Scale measures an earthquake's strength from 0 to 8.9. Each level is 10 times higher than the previous one. No earthquake higher than 8.9 has yet been recorded.

RICHTER SCALE

Level	Strength
0 to 4.3	Mild
4.4 to 4.8	Moderate
4.9 to 6.2	Intermediate
6.3 to 7.3	Severe
7.4 to 8.9	Catastrophic

BIGGEST EARTHQUAKES

Richter level	Location	Date
8.9	**Colombia**	1906
8.9	**Japan,** Morioka	1933
8.75	**Portugal,** Lisbon	1755
8.7	**India,** Assam	1897
8.5	**USA,** Alaska	1964
8.3–8.6	**USA,** Alaska	1899
8.3	**Bolivia**	1994
8.0–8.3	**USA,** Missouri	1811
8.2	**China,** Tangshan	1976
8.1	**Mexico,** Mexico City	1985
7.8	**Turkey**	1999
7.7–8.25	**USA,** San Francisco	1906

EARTH'S OCEANS

Ocean	Area	Average depth
Pacific	166,242,500 sq km	4,188 m
Atlantic	86,557,800 sq km	3,735 m
Indian	73,427,795 sq km	3,872 m
Arctic	13,230,000 sq km	1,038 m

EARTH'S DEEPEST SEA TRENCHES

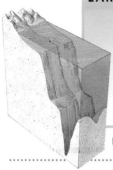

Trench	Ocean	Depth
Marianas	Pacific	10,924 m
Tonga	Pacific	10,800 m
Philippine	Pacific	10,497 m
Kermadec	Pacific	10,047 m
Bonin	Pacific	9,994 m

Marianas Trench is near the island of Guam.

WAVE HEIGHT SCALE

Number	Description	Wave height
0	Glassy; sea like a mirror	0 m
1	Calm; wavelets; crests do not break	0 to 0.3 m
2	Rippled; large wavelets; some "white horses"	0.3 to 0.6 m
3	Choppy; small waves; frequent "white horses"	0.6 to 1.2 m
4	Very choppy; large waves; many "white horses"	1.2 to 2.4 m
5	Rough; large waves; spray	2.4 to 4 m
6	Very rough; high waves; white foam blows	4 to 6 m
7	High; very high waves; rolling water	6 to 9 m
8	Very high; exceptionally high waves; foaming	9 to 14 m
9	Ultra high; sea completely white; foam; spray	More than 14 m

EARTH'S LARGEST ISLANDS

Island	Ocean	Area
Greenland	Atlantic/Arctic oceans	2,131,600 sq km
New Guinea	Pacific Ocean	790,000 sq km
Borneo	Pacific Ocean	737,000 sq km
Madagascar	Indian Ocean	587,000 sq km
Baffin Island	Arctic Ocean	508,000 sq km

Icebergs break off from glaciers along the coast of Greenland.

EARTH'S LONGEST RIVERS

River	Countries	Length
Nile	Tanzania/Uganda/Sudan/Egypt	6,670 km
Amazon	Peru/Brazil	6,440 km
Chang Jiang	China	6,379 km
Mississippi-Missouri	USA	5,971 km
Yenisey-Angara-Selenga	Mongolia/Russia	5,540 km
Huang He (Yellow River)	China	5,464 km

The longest rivers in each continent.

Nile, Africa
Amazon, South America
Chang Jiang, Asia
Mississippi-Missouri, North America
Murray-Darling, Australasia (3,750 km)
Volga, Europe (3,531 km)

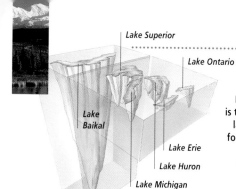

Lake Superior

Lake Ontario

Lake Baikal

Lake Erie

Lake Huron

Lake Michigan

At 1,637 m deep, Lake Baikal (Russia) is the world's deepest lake. It is more than four times as deep as Lake Superior, the deepest of the five Great Lakes.

EARTH'S LARGEST LAKES

Lake	Location	Average area	Average depth
Caspian Sea	Asia	372,000 sq km	995 m
Lake Superior	North America	82,103 sq km	405 m
Lake Victoria	Africa	69,485 sq km	82 m
Lake Huron	North America	59,570 sq km	229 m
Lake Michigan	North America	57,757 sq km	281 m

EARTH'S HIGHEST WATERFALLS

Waterfall	Country	Height
Angel Falls	Venezuela	979 m
Tugela	South Africa	947 m
Utigård	Norway	800 m
Mongefossen	Norway	774 m
Yosemite	USA	739 m

The Angel Falls waterfall is formed as the Rio Churun river plunges over a sheer drop.

EARTH'S GEOLOGICAL TIMESCALE

Era	Period	Epoch	Began
Cenozoic (recent life)	Quaternary	Holocene	10,000 years ago
		Pleistocene	1.6 million years ago
	Tertiary	Pliocene	5 million years ago
		Miocene	23 million years ago
		Oligocene	35 million years ago
		Eocene	56 million years ago
		Palaeocene	65 million years ago
Mesozoic (middle life)	Cretaceous	–	146 million years ago
	Jurassic	–	208 million years ago
	Triassic	–	250 million years ago
Palaeozoic (ancient life)	Permian	–	290 million years ago
	Carboniferous	–	362 million years ago
	Devonian	–	408 million years ago
	Silurian	–	439 million years ago
	Ordovician	–	510 million years ago
	Cambrian	–	550 million years ago
	Precambrian	–	4.56 billion years ago

Dinosaurs lived and died during the Mesozoic era of the Earth's history.

Glossary

abrasion Wearing away of part of the Earth's surface.

abyssal plain A flat region of the ocean floor.

acid rain Rain that is more acidic than usual due to harmful chemicals.

atmosphere The blanket of gases around the Earth.

atoll Ring of coral reef that encloses an area of water.

aurora A display of changing coloured lights in the sky, near one of the magnetic poles.

axis An imaginary line through the Earth around which the planet spins.

biosphere All of the habitats on Earth.

billion One thousand million.

black smoker Chimneylike stacks of minerals on the ocean floor through which hot water gushes.

canyon A steep-sided river valley.

climate The average weather in a place over time.

continent A vast land area.

continental drift The way the continents slowly move around the globe.

continental shelf The area of ocean floor closest to land.

core The metallic centre of the Earth.

crust The rocky outer layer that forms a thin "skin" over the surface of the Earth.

crystals Minerals that have recognisable shapes.

delta A build-up of sand and silt where a river slows down and drops its load as it enters a lake or the ocean.

desert An area with little or no rainfall.

dune A mound of sand.

earthquake A shaking of the ground.

ecosystem A community of living things and their environment.

epicentre The point on the Earth's surface directly above the focus of an earthquake.

equator An imaginary line that divides the Earth into two halves between the poles.

erosion The process that wears away material by wind, water and ice action.

evaporation The process by which a liquid is changed into a vapour or a gas when heated.

fault A crack in the Earth's crust.

fjord A long, deep and narrow inlet from the sea.

focus The point from which an earthquake starts.

fossil The remains or shape of an animal or plant preserved in rock.

fossil fuel A naturally occurring fuel, such as coal, oil and gas, formed from the remains of organic materials.

front The boundary between two masses of air of different temperatures.

fumarole A hole in the Earth's crust through which steam and gases escape.

galaxy A vast cluster of stars, gas and dust in space held together by gravity.

geyser A spring that shoots out hot water and steam.

glacier A mass of slow-moving ice on land made from compressed snow.

global warming The warming of the atmosphere due to pollution.

greenhouse effect The warming of the Earth caused by gases in the atmosphere.

habitat The surroundings in which an animal lives, including climate, water and plants.

hemisphere One half of a sphere. The Earth is divided by the equator into the northern hemisphere and the southern hemisphere.

ice core A sample of ice taken for scientific study.

ice sheet A thick layer of ice that covers a landmass.

iceberg A block of ice floating in the sea.

igneous rock A rock formed by the cooling and hardening of magma, or lava.

latitude Imaginary lines that run around the Earth parallel to the equator.

lava Molten rock from a volcano that turns solid when it cools.

longitude Imaginary lines that run up and down the Earth from pole to pole.

magma Molten rock in the Earth's mantle.

magnetic field An invisible force that surrounds and cloaks the Earth with magnetism.

magnetic pole One of two ends of the Earth's magnetic field.

magnetosphere The zone around the Earth occupied by the Earth's magnetic field.

mantle The rocky middle layer of the Earth.

map projection A way of drawing the curved surface of the Earth on to a flat map.

meander A curve in the course of a river.

metamorphic rock A rock formed when igneous or sedimentary rocks are altered by heat and pressure.

mid-ocean ridge A mountain range under the ocean.

mineral A natural substance in the Earth's crust that has a definite chemical composition and does not come from animals or plants.

moraine Boulders, rock and clay carried inside a glacier.

niche The lifestyle a living thing has within a habitat.

oasis A moist area in a desert where the water table reaches the surface.

ocean trench A deep channel in the floor of the ocean.

ore A type of mineral from which metal is extracted.

photosynthesis The process by which plants use sunlight to produce their food, giving off oxygen as a result.

plate One of the giant slabs of rock that forms the crust.

poles The two ends of the Earth's axis.

precipitation Deposits of water from the atmosphere which reach the ground, such as rain, hail and snow.

pyroclast Fragments of rock produced in volcanic eruptions.

radiosonde Instruments used to collect and transmit information from the atmosphere or underwater.

rift valley A valley formed by the sinking of a piece of land between two parallel faults.

seamount A mountain under the sea.

sea ice Ice that floats on the surface of the sea.

sediment Any solid material carried away from its place of origin and dumped by water, ice or wind.

sedimentary rock A rock formed from the debris of other rocks.

seismic wave A shock wave from the focus of an earthquake.

seismograph A machine for measuring the size of an earthquake.

solar system Everything that orbits the Sun.

stalactite A long, thin piece of calcium carbonate hanging down from the roof of a cave.

stalagmite A column of calcium carbonate growing up from the floor of a cave.

thermal A rising current, or large bubble, of warm air.

tides The rise and fall of the oceans.

trade winds Steady winds in the tropics blowing from the northeast in the northern hemisphere and the southeast in the southern hemisphere.

tsunami A giant sea wave caused by an underwater earthquake.

universe Everything that exists.

valley A broad depression between high ground, usually with a river flowing along the bottom.

volcano A mountain, usually cone-shaped, built up by deposits of lava during an eruption.

water table The level in the ground below which it is full of water.

water vapour Water in the form of an invisible gas.

weathering The gradual breaking down of rocks on the Earth's surface by rain, wind, heat or frost.

wind Moving air.

Index

Note: Page numbers in *italic* refer to captions to illustrations. Main references are in **bold**.

A

a'a lava 62
abrasion 48
abyssal plains 26
acid rain **90**
Africa 60, *103*, 104
air 72, **82**
air masses **75**
air pressure **72**
Albert, Lake *55*
algae 17
Amazon River *102, 109*
amber 33
Antarctica *28*, 60–61, 99, 104
anthracite coal 86
aqueducts 85
Arabian Desert *103*, 105
arches *59*
Arctic *28*
ash 62, 63
Asia *45*, 60, *103*, 104
atmosphere 15, **16**, 17, 77, 82, 84, **90**
atolls *43*
aurora australis 15

B

aurora borealis **15**
auroras **15**
Australian Desert *103*, 105
avalanches 67
axis *13*, 28

bacteria 17
Baffin Island *102*, 109
Baikal, Lake 55, *103*, 110
ball lightning 79
barchan dunes 59, *59*
Big Bang 10
biosphere **88**
Biosphere Project 89, *89*
bituminous coal 86
black smokers **27**
bombs 63
Borneo *103*, 109
breezes 73
buttes 58, *59*

C

cacti 61, *61*
canyons 53
carbon dioxide 16, 17, 82, 83
Caspian Sea *103*, 110
caves **56–57**, 89, **105**
Chang Jiang River *103, 109*
cinder 63

cirrus clouds **76**
clay 35
climate 70
climate zones **70–71**
clouds 10, *74, 75*, **76–77**, 78–79
coal **86**, 87
coastal features **40**
coasts **40**
Colorado River *51*, *53*
columns 58
composite volcano 63
condensation *76*, 84
continental drift **22–23**
continental shelf 26
continents 22, *23*, 26, 42, **104**
copper *33*
coral 43
coral polyps *43*
coral reef 43, *43*
core **20**
crater lake 54
crust 10, **20–21**, 22–23, 24, 30, 44, 52, 53, 54, 55, 62, 66
crystals **32**
crystal systems *32*
cumulus clouds *76*, 79

D

deltas 51, *51*

deserts **58–61**, 105
diamonds 32, *32*,
   33

E

earthquakes *24*,
   66–67, 97, *107*
earthworms **34**
ecosystems **88**, 89,
   89
Edward, Lake *55*
emeralds 32
environment 90
epicentre 66, *67*
equator 12–13, 16,
   70, 94
Erie, Lake *102*, *110*
erosion 40, **41**, *41*,
   42, 49
erosion lake 54
evaporation 84
Everest, Mount 44,
   103, 104

F

fault lines **53**
faults 53, *53*, 45,
   66
fjords 52, *52*
flood plains 50, *50*
focus 66
forests 89
forked lightning 79
fossil formation
   30–31
fossil fuels **86**, 87
fossils 23, **30–31**
Foucault, Jean 12
fronts **74–75**, *74*,
   75

fumaroles 65

G

galaxies 8, 9
gas 87
gems **32**
geological timescale
   111
geysers 65, *65*
glaciers 29, **46–47**,
   46, 48, 52, *52*
   56, 105
global warming **91**
Gobi Desert *61*,
   103, 105
gold 33
Gondwana **22–23**
gorges **49**
grabens **53**
Grand Canyon 53
gravity 11, 38
Great Rift Valley **55**
greenhouse gases
   91, *91*
Greenland *102*, 109

H

habitats **89**
hamadas *59*
Hawaii 43, 44
heat 9, 12, **86**
hemispheres 73
Himalayas 45
Huang He River ***103***,
   109
Huron, Lake *102*,
   110

I

icebergs 29, *29*, *108*

ice breaker *29*
ice cores 99, *99*
ice crystals **76**, 77
ice sheet 29, 99
igneous rock 31,
   31
islands **42–43**, **109**

J

jet 33
Jupiter 8

K

K2 104
Kivu, Lake *55*

L

lagoon 43
lakes **54–55**, 85,
   89, 90, 110
land breeze 73
landslides 67
lapilli 63
latitude *94*
Laurasia **22–23**
lava 56, 62
light 9, 12, **86**
lightning **78**, 79
lignite coal 86
longitude *94*
Lystrosaurus 23

M

Madagascar *103*,
   109
magma **20**, 22, *24*,
   25, 31, 43, 45,
   62
magnetic field
   14–15

magnetic poles **15**, 28

mantle **20**, 22, **62**

maps **94**

Marianas Trench 21, **27**, 108

Mars *8*

Mauna Kea 44

meanders 50, *54*

Mercalli Earthquake Intensity Scale **107**

Mercury *8*

mesas 58

metamorphic rock 31

Michigan, Lake *102*, 110

mid-ocean ridges *24*, 26

Milky Way 9, *9*

minerals **30**, 32, 34, 50, 85

Mississippi-Missouri rivers *102*, **109**

Moon **38–39**, *39*

moons 8

mountains 24, *24*, **44**, 60, 89, **104**

mud pools 65

Murray-Darling rivers *103*, **109**

N

Neptune 9

New Guinea *103*, 109

Nile River *103*, **109**

nitrogen 16

North Pole 14–15, **28**, *28*

Nyasa, Lake *54*

O

oases 60

occluded fronts **75**

ocean ridges 25

oceans 10, 17, **26–27**, 38, 89, 102–103, **108**

ocean trenches *24*, 25–26, 99, **108**

oil **86**, 87, *90*

Ontario, Lake 102, *110*

ores **33**

oxbow lakes 50, *50*, 54

oxygen 16–17, **82**, 83

P

pahoehoe lava **62**, *62*

Pangaea *22*

Patagonian Desert *102*, 105

peat 86

Philippines, the 27, *63*

photosynthesis 82–83

pillow lava **62**

Pinatubo, Mount *63*

planets **8**, *8–9*, 11

plates 22, **24–25**, 42, 43, 45, **53**, *62*, 66

plunge pool 49, *49*

Pluto *9*

polar regions **70**

poles 12–13, 15, 16, 28, **71**, **72**, 75, 91

pollution **90**

polyps *43*

potholes **49**

precipitation **77**, 79, *82*

precious stones **32–33**

pumice **63**

pyroclasts 63

R

radiosondes **97**, *97*

rain 10, 17, **54**, 76, 77, 96

rainforests 83, *83*, **88**, 89

reservoir 85

respiration 82

Richter Scale **107**

rift valley **53**, 53

rivers **48–51**, *52, 54*, 85, **109**

rock **30–31**

rock cycle **30**

rock types 31

Rukwa, Lake *54*

rubies 32, *33*

S

Sahara Desert 61, *103*, 105

salt 85, *85*

San Andreas Fault 25

sand 35, 58–59, 85

sand dunes *40*, **59**, *59*

satellites 98, *98*

Saturn *8*

sea **84**, 87

sea breeze 73

sea ice **29**, *29*

seamounts 26

seasons **12**

sea water *85*

sea waves **38**

sedimentary rock 31, 44

seif dunes 59, *59*

seismograph 97, *97*

semiprecious stones 32

sheet lightning 79

shell 33

shock or seismic waves 20, 67, *67*

silt 35

snow 46, **47**, **76**, 77

snowflakes **47**

soil **34–35**

solar system **8**, *11*

solar wind 14, 15

Sonoran Desert *61*

South Pole 13, 14–15, **28**, *28*

stalactites **57**, *57*

stalagmites **57**, *57*

star dunes 59, *59*

storms **78–79**

stratus clouds **76**

submarine canyons **53**

submersibles 26

Sun 8, **9**, *9*, 11–14, 16, **38–39**, **70**, **71**, 77, 84

Superior, Lake *102*, 110

Surtsey *43*

T

Taklimakan Desert 61

Tanganyika, Lake *54*

temperate areas **70**

thermals 77

thunder **78**, *78*, 79

thunderstorms 78–79

tide cycle **38–39**

trade winds 73, *73*

transverse dunes 59, *59*

tides **38–39**, *39*

tropics **70**, *71*, 75

troposphere 16, *16*

tsunami 67

Turkana, Lake *55*

U

universe 8–10

Uranus *9*

V

valleys 46–47, 48, 50, **52–53**

vents 27, **62**

Venus *8*

Victoria, Lake 55, *103*, *110*

volcanic eruption *43*

Volcanic Explosivity

Index **106**

volcanic islands 43

volcanoes 42–43, 44, 54, **62–64**, **106**

Volgar River *103*, *109*

W

wadis 58

water **84**, **85**, *85*

water cycle **84**, **90**

water droplets **76**, 90

waterfalls **49**, 110

water treatment plants *85*

water vapour **76**, 77, 84, **90**

wave height scale 108

waves **38**

weather **12**, 16, **70**, **74**, **78**, 96–97

weather balloons 97

weather buoys 96

weather stations 96

wind 38, 58–59, **72–73**, 77

Y

Yenisey-Angara-Selenga rivers 103, 109

Useful addresses

Information on Earth-related subjects can be obtained from the following organisations and web sites.

AGRICULTURE AND INDUSTRY
The United Nations Information Centre, Millbank Tower, 21–24 Millbank, London SW1P 4QH, UK

ENVIRONMENT
The National Environment Research Council Schools Programme Polaris House, North Star Avenue, Swindon SN2 1EU, UK

Web sites

CAVES
www.goodearth.com/virtmap.html
Virtual Cave

GEOGRAPHY AND EARTH SCIENCE
www.nationalgeographic.com
National Geographic Magazine
www.nasa.gov
NASA
www.discovery.com
Discovery Channel
www.cotf.edu/ete/modules/msese/explorer.html
Earth Science Explorer

GEOLOGY
www.usgs.gov
US Geological Survey

GLACIERS
www.glacier.rice.edu
Glaciers

OCEANS
www.whoi.edu
Woods Hole Oceanographic Institute

RAINFORESTS
www.EnchantedLearning.com/subjects/rainforest
Zoom Rainforest

BIOMES AND ECOSYSTEMS
http://mbgnet.mobot.org/sets/index.htm
The Evergreen Project

VOLCANOES AND EARTHQUAKES
http://volcano.und.nodak.edu
Volcano World
www.earthquake.org
Global Earthquake Response Center

WEATHER
www.met-office.gov.uk
The UK Meteorological Office
www.nws.noaa.gov
National Weather Service

Acknowledgements

l = left; r = right; b = bottom; t = top; c = centre

ILLUSTRATIONS
Richard Bonson: 17, 30–31b, 34–35c; **William Donahoe**: 54–55; **Eugene Fleury**: 28, 32, 70, 73tr, 75cr, 83, 94b, 95t, 102–103; **Mike Foster**: 16, 94c; **Lee Gibbons**: 9c; **Gary Hincks**: 10, 25, 26–27b, 27, 29, 31c, 35tr, 42–43, 44b, 48–49, 50–51, 52–53, 55t, 56–57, 63, 64–65, 74–75b, 76l, 84–85, 91l, 99, 104–105, 106, 108–109, 110; **Rob Jakeway**: 11; **Aziz Khan**: 14–15, 30c, 38–39; **Mainline Design**: 22–23c, 67r; **Janos Marffy**: 8–9b, 38l; **Jonathon Potter**: 47 br; **Eric Robson**: 23t, 61, 88–89t, 111; **Michael Roffe**: 91r (insets); **Colin Salmon**: 3, 20–21, 82; **Martin Sanders**: 96–97b, 97; **Peter Sarson**: 86–87, 107; **Peter Sarson/Richard Chasemore**: 12–13, 45t, 47rt, 54l, 58c, 60, 64–67, 71tr, 72–73b, 77, 78–79, 96c; **Roger Stewart**: 24, 26c, 40–41, 44–45c, 46–47, 58–59b, 62, 94–95c; **David Webb** 88b; **Colin Woolf**: 71c.

PHOTOGRAPHS
4t Digital Vision, 4tc Jean-Paul Ferrero/ Ardea, 4bc Gregory Dimijian/ Science Photo Library, 4b Digital Vision; 5t F. S. Westmorland/ Science Photo Library, 5c Digital Vision, 5b Daniel J. Cox/ Oxford Scientific Films; 6/7 Digital Vision; 9t Susan McCartney/ Science Photo Library, 9b David Malin/ Royal Observatory Edinburgh; 10 Digital Vision; 13 Tony Stone Images; 15 Astrofoto/ Bruce Coleman; 18/19 Jean-Paul Ferrero/ Ardea; 25, 29t Corbis, 29b Tui de Roy/ Oxford Scientific Films; 31l GeoScience Features, 31c, r; 32 Breck P. Kent/ Oxford Scientific Films, 33tl E. R. Degginger/ Oxford Scientific Films, 33tr Nick Gordon/ Ardea, 33tc, bc Jim Frazier/ Oxford Scientific Films; 33bl Breck P. Kent/ Oxford Scientific Films, 33br P.J. Green/ Ardea; 34 Jean-Paul Ferrero/ Ardea; 36/37 Gregory Dimijian/ Science Photo Library; 41, 42 Corbis; 43 Bruce Coleman; 51 Corbis; 53 Gavin Hellier/ Robert Harding Picture Library; 57 Corbis; 59 PowerStock/ Zefa; 61 Paul Harris/ Royal Geographical Society; 62 Corbis; 63 Bourseiller - I & V/ Planet Earth Pictures; 65 David Halpern/ Science Photo Library; 66/67 Popperfoto; 74/75t Jacobs/ Robert Harding Picture Library, 74/75b John E. Swedberg/ Ardea; 79 Adam Jones/ Planet Earth Pictures; 80/81 F.S. Westmorland/ Science Photo Library; 83 Will & Deni McIntyre/ Science Photo library; 85 Ronald Torns/ Oxford Scientific Films; 86/87 Ken Vaughan/ Planet Earth Pictures; 89 Peter Menzel/ Science Photo Library; 90 Mike Hill/ Oxford Scientific Films; 92/93, 95 Digital Vision; 97l, r John Stockwell/ US Geological National Earthquake Information Centre, Golden, Colorado; 98l, r Digital Vision; 99 J. G. Paren/ Science Photo Library; 100/101 Daniel J. Cox/ Oxford Scientific Films.